animal
fact
files

INSECTS

ROD PRESTON-MAFHAM
KEN PRESTON-MAFHAM

with Andrew Campbell
and Amy-Jane Beer

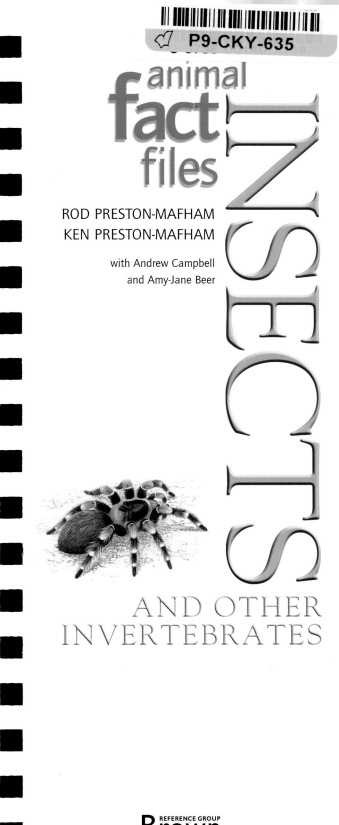

AND OTHER
INVERTEBRATES

REFERENCE GROUP
Brown

The Brown Reference Group plc
8 Chapel Place
Rivington Street
London EC2A 3DQ
www.brownreference.com

ISBN 184044195X

Editorial Director: Lindsey Lowe

Project Director: Graham Bateman

Art Director: Steve McCurdy

Editor: Virginia Carter

Artists: Denys Ovenden, Richard Lewington

Printed in China

Contents

Introduction

All life on Earth originated in the primeval seas some 4,000 million years ago. After eons of evolution a dizzying array of life has evolved. While the most obvious and most recently evolved (in relative terms) are the fish, amphibians, reptiles, birds, and mammals, there remains a wealth of other life forms that evolved long before these groups. Often small or invisible to the naked eye, the number of such species far surpasses that of the more obvious and familiar species. There are, for example, at least one million species of insects known, and the number is rising daily.

Animal Fact File: Insects and other Invertebrates looks at all the main groups of invertebrate life. Invertebrates are defined as those animals that do not have a backbone: in other words, all animal life except fish, amphibians, reptiles, birds, and mammals.

Very little links the diverse forms and lifestyles of the groups covered here. Firstly, we look at four groups (phyla) of single-celled life, which form the kingdom Protista. Most are microscopic in size. Some have characteristics of true animals, some of plants, and some of both.

Our journey then takes us into the realm of true animals, kingdom Animalia. Kingdom Animalia contains 34 phyla, only one of which (Chordata) contains animals with backbones. Under the heading "Simple Animals" (see page 3) there are articles on a number of the more familiar invertebrate phyla (such as sponges and flatworms) or subgroups of phyla (such as jellyfish, sea anemones, and corals). In reality, none of these animals is truly simple. There is nothing simple about a sponge—a creature that is rooted to the spot and lacks even rudimentary organs yet is able to process thousands of liters of water a day in order to filter out food particles.

The largest proportion of articles in this book covers the phylum Arthropoda—the arthropods. They include the insects, millipedes, spiders, and crustaceans. The name "arthropod" is derived from the Greek, and literally means "jointed limb." However, the most important feature (and what sets them apart from other groups of animals) is the tough outer cuticle that forms the external skeleton. It covers all the internal organs as well as all the muscles that work the various external appendages. Arthropods molt the cuticle at various times to allow the body to grow.

The Arthropoda is sometimes divided into two sections —the Biramia and the Uniramia. The Biramia includes just one subphylum, the Crustacea, whose appendages, antennae, and limbs are all made up of two branches. They are mainly aquatic creatures and include the crabs, lobsters, barnacles, prawns, and shrimps. All the remaining subphyla are included in the Uniramia because their appendages are unbranched. Although they include aquatic species, the majority of them are terrestrial. The exceptions are the sea spiders, Pycnogonida, which are exclusively marine. Members of the subphylum Chelicerata (spiders and scorpions) have four pairs of legs, while the Myriapoda (centipedes and millipedes) all have more than five pairs of legs. The Hexapoda have just three pairs of legs and include the most successful group, the insects. In this book there are articles about many families of insects, arranged into their major groups such as beetles, true bugs, butterflies and moths, and wasps, ants, and bees.

The last stop on our journey through invertebrate life takes in two primarily aquatic phyla—the Mollusca (mollusks) and the Echinodermata (echinoderms). Mollusks usually have a shell of some sort and are either snail-, slug-, clam-, or squidlike in form. The exclusively marine echinoderms (starfish, sea urchins, and sea cucumbers) are either star-shaped or round and protected by a spiny skin.

Naming Animals

In order to discuss particular animals names are needed for the different kinds. For example, most people would regard the American monarch butterfly as one kind of butterfly and the cabbage white as another. All American monarchs look alike. They breed together and produce offspring the same as themselves. This popular distinction corresponds closely to the zoologist's definition of a species. All American monarchs belong to one species, and all cabbage whites to another.

Many animals have different names in different languages or more than one in a single language. Therefore, zoologists use an internationally recognized system for naming species, consisting of two-word names, usually in Latin or Greek. The American monarch butterfly is called *Danaus plexippus*, and the cabbage white is *Pieris rapae*.

The first word, for example, *Danaus,* is the genus (a group of similar species), which would include other monarchlike butterflies, such as the American queen. The second word, for example, *plexippus,* indicates the species in the genus, distinguishing it from the American queen, *Danaus gilippus*.

Rank	Scientific name	Common name
Kingdom	Animalia	Animals
Phylum	Arthropoda	Animals with an external skeleton and jointed limbs
Class	Insecta	Six-legged arthropods
Order	Lepidoptera	Butterflies and moths
Family	Danaidae	Milkweed butterflies
Genus	*Danaus*	
Species	*plexippus*	Monarch butterfly

The kingdom Animalia is subdivided into phyla, classes, orders, families, genera, and species. Above is the classification for the monarch butterfly.

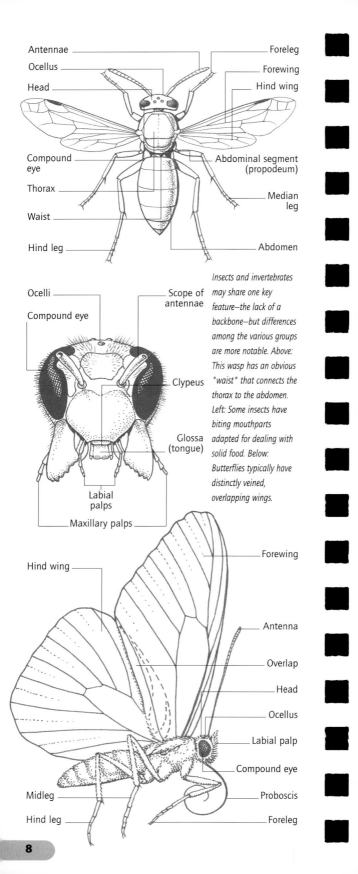

Antennae
Ocellus
Head
Compound eye
Thorax
Waist
Hind leg

Foreleg
Forewing
Hind wing
Abdominal segment (propodeum)
Median leg
Abdomen

Ocelli
Compound eye
Scope of antennae
Clypeus
Glossa (tongue)
Labial palps
Maxillary palps

Insects and invertebrates may share one key feature—the lack of a backbone—but differences among the various groups are more notable. Above: This wasp has an obvious "waist" that connects the thorax to the abdomen. Left: Some insects have biting mouthparts adapted for dealing with solid food. Below: Butterflies typically have distinctly veined, overlapping wings.

Hind wing

Forewing
Antenna
Overlap
Head
Ocellus
Labial palp
Compound eye
Proboscis
Foreleg

Midleg
Hind leg

The same scientific names are recognized the world over. In this way the system allows precision and avoids confusion. However, it is possible for a species to have (or have had) two or more scientific names—it may have been described and named at different times without the zoologists realizing it was a single species. Usually when such a discrepancy is discovered, the first name takes priority.

As we have seen earlier, it is necessary to make statements about larger groups of animals. Classification makes this possible. In the example of the monarch butterfly all species that are similar to monarch butterflies are grouped in the family Danaidae, the milkweed butterflies; all butterfly and moth families are grouped in the order Lepidoptera; all lepidopterans and other insect orders are grouped in the class Insecta; and all insects and other animal classes that have an external skeleton and jointed limbs are contained within the phylum Arthropoda.

About this Book

In *Animal Fact File: Insects and other Invertebrates* you will find illustrated articles on 210 groups of insects and other invertebrates. Each article follows a fixed structure. The color-coded header strip denotes the category (see pages 3 to 5) to which each animal belongs and gives its common name. There follows an illustration of a typical animal from the group, along with a caption specific to that animal. The fact panel then gives the scientific name of the animal in question and other taxonomic information. The sections that follow describe different features of the animals and their lifestyles.

Spiders form a large group within the subphylum Chelicerata. Unlike insects, they have two regions of the body rather than three, and normally eight legs instead of an insect's six.

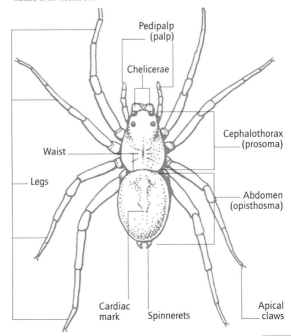

Pedipalp (palp)

Chelicerae

Cephalothorax (prosoma)

Waist

Legs

Abdomen (opisthosma)

Cardiac mark

Spinnerets

Apical claws

Flagellates

Chlamydomonas is a plantlike flagellate that swims through water by beating a pair of hairlike flagella.

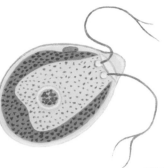

Photosynthesis takes place in the horseshoe-shaped chloroplast. It is one of the commonest flagellates found in damp places throughout the world. Size microscopic up to 0.009 inches (0.024 mm) long.

Chlamydomonas sp.

Common name
Flagellates

Subphylum Mastigophora

Phylum Sarcomastigophora

Kingdom Protista

Number of species About 1,500

Size Most are a few thousandths of an inch; some are just large enough to be seen with the naked eye

Key features Highly variable single-celled organisms; all have at least 1 long flagellum (organ of locomotion) at some stage in life cycle

Habits Many live as commensals, parasites, or symbionts within other animals at some stage in life cycle

Breeding Highly varied and little understood; can be asexual or sexual with varying degrees of differentiation between male and female gametes (sex cells)

Diet Plantlike flagellates produce at least some of their own food by photosynthesis; others feed by engulfing prey items or absorbing nutrients from a host

Habitat Mostly aquatic when not inside host

Distribution Worldwide

Amebas and Allies

One of the larger amebas, *Ameba proteus* is often observed in schools by students learning about simple animals. The species is aptly named—Proteus was a Greek god who could assume various forms. Size up to 0.2 inches (5 mm).

Ameba proteus

Common name Amebas, forams, heliozoans, radiolarians

Subphylum Sarcodina

Phylum Sarcomastigophora

Kingdom Protista

Number of species About 11,500

Size Mostly microscopic, but some amebas reach 0.2 in (5 mm), and some forams grow to 1 in (2.5 cm) or more; radiolarians may form colonies 8 in (20 cm) long

Key features Asymmetrical or spherical protists lacking flagellae, but with variable pseudopods; may be naked or secrete a proteinaceous or siliceous shell, test, or skeleton

Habits Aquatic, free living, occasionally parasitic

Breeding Sexual by conjugation or asexual by fission or schizogony

Diet Feed by engulfing other organisms, mainly bacteria and organic matter

Habitat Wherever there is moisture; in oceans, rivers, lakes, puddles, soil, caves, and in and around multicellular plants and animals; several species have been collected from the earth's upper atmosphere

Distribution Worldwide

Ciliates

Paramecium is surrounded by a tough coating with numerous cilia. It also has a distinct furrow leading to the cytostome, or cell mouth.
Length about 0.02 inches (0.5 mm).

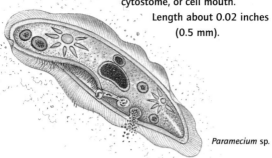

Paramecium sp.

Common name Ciliates

Phylum Ciliophora

Kingdom Protista

Number of species About 8,000 known, with many more yet to be described

Size Generally microscopic, from a few microns to 0.1 in (3 mm) in length

Key features Single-celled organisms with two distinct types of nuclei and external cilia; internal structure may be very complex

Habits Mostly free living; occasionally parasitic; many have resistant cyst phase

Breeding Mostly asexual by binary fission; no males or females—sexual reproduction involves conjugation of compatible cell types

Diet Mostly bacteria that are engulfed and digested in cell vacuoles

Habitat Mainly fresh water

Distribution Worldwide

Malaria

Four *Plasmodium* species are responsible for causing malaria in humans. The disease has been eradicated in the United States, but in the developing world control measures have had little effect to date.

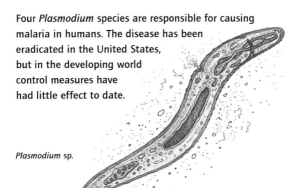

Plasmodium sp.

Common name Malaria

Phylum Apicomplexa (formerly Sporozoa)

Kingdom Protista

Number of species About 4,000 described to date

Size Mostly a few microns, occasionally up to 0.4 in (10 mm) long

Key features Single cells, usually elongate; tips of the cell contain a complex of filaments

Habits Parasitic

Breeding Life cycles often involve sexual and asexual phases and multiple hosts

Diet Nutrients absorbed from host

Habitat Bodies of other animals, either inside or alongside host cells

Distribution Worldwide, especially prevalent in tropical regions

Sponges

Columns of the brown tube sponge, *Agelas conifera*, rise from the seabed like smokestacks. This sponge is found in seas around the Bahamas, the Caribbean, and Florida. Growing up to 36 inches (90 cm) tall, brown tube sponges are sometimes home to small fish that live inside their hollow core.

Brown tube sponge
(*Agelas conifera*)

Common name
Sponges

Phylum Porifera

Number of species About 5,000

Size Variable, from 0.1 in (2.5 mm) to 40 in (100 cm) or more in height; occasionally over 10 ft (3 m) across

Key features Simple, radially symmetrical but irregularly shaped animals; made up of largely undifferentiated (nonspecialized) tissues around a system of channels and chambers through which water can flow; mostly colorful, in shades of red, orange, purple, yellow, and green; occasionally dull and inconspicuous

Habits Nonmoving, usually attached to hard substratum

Breeding Asexual by budding or production of gemmules (cell packets), or sexual with internal fertilization and direct development into small adults

Diet Small bacteria, protists, and particles of organic material

Habitat Mostly marine at all depths; some freshwater species exist

Distribution Worldwide

Comb Jellies

Pleurobrachia pileus is common in open water, but is occasionally found stranded in rock pools. Sometimes vast numbers congregate together. It can be found in the Atlantic, Mediterranean, English Channel, and the North and Baltic Seas. Length up to 1.2 inches (3 cm).

Pleurobrachia pileus

Common name Comb jellies (sea gooseberries, sea walnuts)

Phylum Ctenophora

Number of species About 100

Size 0.2 in (4 mm) to 40 in (100 cm)

Key features Gelatinous, largely translucent body has radial symmetry (some forms also have superimposed bilateral symmetry), bearing 8 rows of comblike structures made up of fused cilia; most species have long trailing tentacles

Habits Free swimming; often rise to surface waters at night

Breeding Sexual reproduction involves the release of gametes by hermaphrodite individuals; fertilized eggs develop into free-swimming cydippid larva that metamorphoses into adult form

Diet Includes crustaceans and other comb jellies; some species trap slow-moving fish

Habitat Open sea

Distribution Worldwide

Hydrozoans

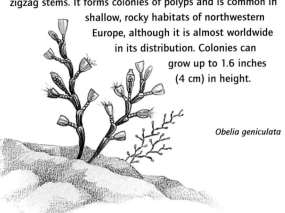

Obelia geniculata is a distinctive species, with slender zigzag stems. It forms colonies of polyps and is common in shallow, rocky habitats of northwestern Europe, although it is almost worldwide in its distribution. Colonies can grow up to 1.6 inches (4 cm) in height.

Obelia geniculata

Common name Hydrozoans, hydroids, hydrocorals, hydras, Portuguese men-of-war

Class Hydrozoa

Phylum Cnidaria

Number of species About 3,000

Size Varies greatly; individual polyps mostly very small, but hydroid colonies can be up to 6 in (15 cm) tall; some deep-sea species produce solitary polyps over 6 ft (1.8 m) long; floating Portuguese man-of-war colonies can be several feet long including tentacles

Key features Very varied group; in all cases mesoglea lacks cells; stinging cells are on the outside of the body, never inside; gonads shed gametes externally; basic forms include solitary and colonial polyps with or without a hard skeleton and some small medusae

Habits Live in open seas, attached directly to substratum

Breeding Asexual by budding (may lead to separate individuals or expansion into a colony); sexual reproduction occurs in medusa phase or in gonophores (reproductive zooids) attached to polyp colony

Diet Small particles of food collected from the water; prey animals killed by stinging cnidocytes

Habitat Aquatic, mostly marine; some species (notably hydras) live in fresh water

Distribution Worldwide

Jellyfish

The adult medusa of the moon jellyfish, *Aurelia aurita*. The moon jellyfish has global distribution and can survive a wide range of sea temperatures. Its sting causes an itchy rash. Diameter 10 inches (25 cm).

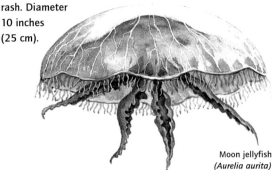

Moon jellyfish
(*Aurelia aurita*)

Common name Jellyfish (sea jellies)

Class　Scyphozoa and Cubozoa

Phylum Cnidaria

Number of species About 200

Size　Mature medusae measure 0.5 in (13 mm) to 6.5 ft (2 m) in diameter

Key features In most species the predominant form is a saucer-, bell-, or helmet-shaped medusa with fringe of tentacles around the edge or elaborate arms trailing from mouth in center of underside

Habits　Most swim freely in open seas by means of pulsating bell; may migrate vertically to feed in shallower water at night

Breeding Medusae shed gametes via mouth; fertilization takes place in the water; embryos develop via 2 larval stages: The swimming planula larva develops into fixed polyplike scyphistoma larva, from which miniature medusae are produced asexually

Diet　A wide variety of invertebrate prey and some fish killed by stinging cells on tentacles or oral arms

Habitat Marine, mostly open seas, occasionally bottom dwellers

Distribution Worldwide

Sea Anemones

Metridium senile, the frilled anemone, is found from the Arctic to southern California. Large specimens can have 1,000 tentacles. Height up to 18 inches (46 cm). *Actinia equina*, the beadlet anemone, is from the Atlantic and Mediterranean. It is the most common anemone found on northern European rocky shores. Height about 3 inches (7 cm).

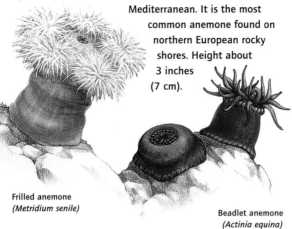

Frilled anemone
(*Metridium senile*)

Beadlet anemone
(*Actinia equina*)

Common name Sea anemones

Order Actinaria

Class Anthozoa (part)

Phylum Cnidaria

Number of species About 1,000

Size Up to 40 in (100 cm) in diameter

Key features Solitary polyps with predominantly 6-fold symmetry; often very colorful

Habits Mostly slow moving with long periods attached to a single spot; may creep, climb, burrow, or swim; solitary

Breeding Sexual reproduction results in planula larva that settles and metamorphoses into miniature polyp; most species also reproduce asexually by binary fission or regeneration from small fragments of tissue

Diet Various invertebrate prey; occasionally snare fish with stinging tentacles; many species receive proportion of nutritional requirements from symbiotic algae

Habitat Marine, from coastal zones to deep oceans

Distribution In all oceans and adjoining seas worldwide

Corals

Colonies of the soft coral *Alcyonium digitatum*, or dead man's fingers, can be found around the coasts of Western Europe. Colonies can grow up to 8 inches (20 cm) in height.

Dead man's fingers
(Alcyonium digitatum)

Common name
Stony corals,
soft corals, horny corals,
sea pens, sea fans

Class Anthozoa (part)

Phylum Cnidaria

Number of species About 5,000

Size Solitary forms up to 20 in (50 cm) in diameter; polyps of colonial forms usually less than 0.2 in (5 mm) in diameter; colonies up to several feet across; entire reefs can extend for miles

Key features Mostly colonial polyps, either soft bodied or overlying a stony skeleton of secreted calcium carbonate; colony may be encrusting or erect, making antler, feather, fan, plate, slipper, or boulder shape; colors include vibrant shades of red, purple, orange, green, and blue or brown and black

Habits Sessile (attached by the substratum); colonial, but compete aggressively for growing space

Breeding Colonies grow by asexual budding; sexual reproduction involves simultaneous shedding of gametes into the water; fertilization leads to development of free-swimming planula larvae that disperse and settle to found new colonies elsewhere

Diet Reef-building (hermatypic) corals gain most of their nutrients from symbiotic algae living inside each polyp; other food, mainly plankton and bacteria, is captured from water by tentacles

Habitat Marine, mostly shallow tropical seas; some specialized corals live in deeper and colder water

Distribution Worldwide, mainly in the tropics

Lampshells

Lingula anatina lies with its shell at the top of a burrow, where it feeds by filtering seawater. The genus *Lingula* is the oldest genus of animal life of which there are still living species and dates back over 425 million years. Length (shell) 0.8–1 inches (2–3 cm).

Lingula anatina

Common name Lampshells

Phylum Brachiopoda

Number of species About 260

Size Shell 0.3 in (8 mm) to 1.5 in (4 cm)

Key features Simple animal with paired convex shells attached at the back end, usually with fleshy stalk; mantle cavity mostly filled with the paired loops of a tentacled feeding structure, the lophophore

Habits Sedentary as adults; live attached to hard substratum or burrow into soft sediment

Breeding Most species have separate males and females; fertilization and larval development take place in the water; a few species brood embryos within their shells

Diet Small particles filtered out of the water, including plankton and detritus

Habitat Marine, from intertidal zones to deep ocean

Distribution Worldwide, but generally in colder water

Moss Animals

Some bryozoans form erect, branching colonies that look rather like fronds of seaweed. The hornwrack, *Flustra foliacea*, is found in Europe. It forms dense beds below the tide line on coarse, rocky shores that are swept by currents, where it often provides shelter for many other invertebrates. It grows to about 8 inches (20 cm) in height.

Hornwrack
(Flustra foliacea)

Common name Moss animals, sea mats

Phylum Bryozoa

Number of species About 5,000

Size   Individual animals about 0.02 in (0.5 mm) long, but colonies may be up to 10 in (25 cm) tall or cover 3 to 4 sq. ft (0.3–0.4 sq. m)

Key features Individual animals (zooids) live within compartment of secreted material; body is dominated by large gut and retractable tentacled feeding structure

Habits Sedentary; colonial

Breeding Mostly hermaphrodite; sexual reproduction results in larvae that settle and reproduce asexually by budding to found new colonies

Diet   Small particles of organic material including algae, zooplankton, and detritus

Habitat Aquatic, mainly marine, attached to substrate such as rocks, algae, and man-made structures at all depths

Distribution Worldwide

Horseshoe Worms

The green phoronid worm, *Phoronopsis viridis*, can be found on mudflats and sands from Oregon to California. Like most horseshoe worms, its body is much longer than its width—in this case 80 times longer. Length 8 inches (20 cm).

Green phoronid worm
(Phoronopsis viridis)

Common name Horseshoe worms

Phylum Phoronida

Number of species 15

Size From 0.2 in (6 mm) to 8 in (20 cm) long

Key features Long, unsegmented wormlike body with large horseshoe- or spiral-shaped crown of retractable tentacles

Habits Sedentary; tube dwelling

Breeding Mostly hermaphrodite; some species brood developing eggs among tentacles; free-swimming larvae are planktonic before settling and metamorphosing into adult form; also reproduce asexually by budding and splitting into two (fission)

Diet Algae, zooplankton, and particles of detritus filtered by lophophore

Habitat Marine, bottom dwelling, mostly tropical or shallow temperate seas with warm water

Distribution Worldwide

Flatworms and Tapeworms

Gliding over rocks and seaweed in shallow seas, the free-swimming candystripe flatworm, *Prostheceraeus vittatus*, is occasionally seen by divers. It lives beneath stones in muddy habitats in the Atlantic Ocean and the North Sea. Length 2 inches (5 cm).

Candystripe flatworm
(Prostheceraeus vittatus)

Common name Flatworms, tapeworms, flukes

Phylum Platyhelminthes

Number of species About 25,000

Size From about 0.001 in (0.03 mm) to 13 ft (4 m); occasionally reach 65 ft (20 m)

Key features Flattened body with front and rear end; no coelom (body cavity), gut often absent or incomplete, or may be finely branched, but with no anus; anterior end may carry simple sense organs such as light-sensitive ocelli

Habits Free living and parasitic, often with several hosts; move by swimming or crawling

Breeding Sexual and asexual, most species hermaphrodite, but some dioecious (having either male or female sexual organs); development may be direct from egg to adult or involve metamorphosis from a free-living larval form; life cycle may involve more than 1 host

Diet Free-living species may be carnivorous or scavenging; parasites feed on body fluids or gut contents of host

Habitat Free-living species are mostly aquatic; some have evolved to live in humid places on land; parasitic species are carried with hosts

Distribution Worldwide

Ribbon Worms

Lineus longissimus is shown here in a typical tangled mass. It is found under stones and rocks on the lower shore and in shallow parts of the North Sea, the Atlantic Ocean, and the Baltic Sea. Length usually up to 16 feet (5m), but occasionally 100 feet (30 m).

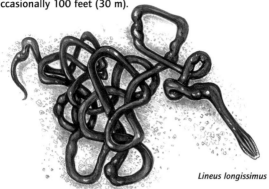

Lineus longissimus

Common name Ribbon worms, proboscis worms

Phylum Nemertea (also known as Rhynchocoela or Nemertini)

Number of species About 1,000 described, but total is probably several times more

Size 0.04 in (1 mm) to 100 ft (30 m) or more

Key features Long, often flattened body; body soft and unsegmented, with complete gut and anus; large projectile proboscis used in feeding may be armed with piercing stylet; body may be colorful with banded pattern

Habits Usually bottom dwelling, often burrowing; occasionally living commensally on mollusk hosts

Breeding Asexual by fission (breaking of the body) and regeneration or sexual with external fertilization; development is directly to adult or indirectly via a larval stage called the pilidium

Diet Most are predatory on worms and other invertebrates; others omnivorous

Habitat Mostly bottom-dwelling marine habitats, but some in fresh water; a few terrestrial species occur in the humid tropics

Distribution Worldwide

Roundworms

Strongyloides is a species of roundworm. Its smooth, tapering body, with no bristles, is typical of the group. Length up to 0.08 inches (2 mm).

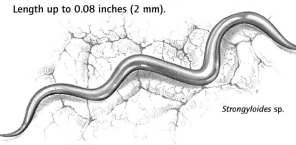

Strongyloides sp.

Common name Roundworms (threadworms)

Phylum Nematoda

Number of species Over 15,000 species described, but total could range into millions

Size Mostly less than 0.02 in (0.5 mm), the largest species reach 43 ft (13 m)

Key features Unsegmented body, circular in cross-section, with tapering ends; gut with anterior mouth and posterior anus running through body cavity (pseudocoel); body sheathed in protein cuticle of varying kinds depending on species

Habits Free-living and parasitic on plants and animals

Breeding Sexes separate in most species; males and females mate, with internal fertilization of eggs; eggs then shed into environment and go through 4 larval instars before reaching maturity

Diet All kinds of organic material, living and dead

Habitat Anywhere with a small amount of free water—oceans, seas, lakes, rivers, soil, and sand; also in ice and hot springs; parasitic species live within almost every other form of multicellular life

Distribution Worldwide—potentially more widespread than any other group of living organisms

Beard Worms

Oligobrachia ivanovi is a beard worm species from the northeastern Atlantic. It is shown partly exposed from its tube. Beard worms are found mainly at great depths. Length over 36 inches (1 m).

Oligobrachia ivanovi

Common name Beard worms

Phylum Pogonophora

Number of species About 150

Size   Most 2 in (5 cm) to 30 in (80 cm) long, some giants grow to about 6.5 ft (1.9 m)

Key features Segmented body largely encased in long chitinous tube; front section bears "beard" of fine tentacles; mouth and gut are absent in adult form

Habits Sessile; tube dwelling

Reproduction Sperm released into the water by males finds its way into the tubes of females; trochophore larvae develop from eggs fertilized inside the tube, then swim free for a short time before settling somewhere close by to begin adult life

Diet   Some organic molecules absorbed from the water, most food is supplied by bacteria living within the animal that produce carbohydrates by the process of chemosynthesis

Habitat Deep ocean, from 330 ft (100 m) to the deepest trenches

Distribution Not fully known, but examples are known from all oceans

Ragworms and Allies

Three representative species of bottom-dwelling polychaete worms, all found in the North Atlantic Ocean. *Eulalia viridis* is up to 6 inches (15 cm) long, *Marphysa sanguinea* grows up to 24 inches (60 cm), and the scale worm, *Harmothoe inibricata,* is just 2 inches (5 cm) in length.

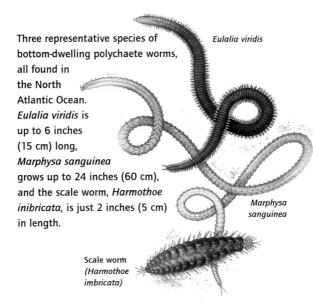

Eulalia viridis

Marphysa sanguinea

Scale worm (*Harmothoe imbricata*)

Common name Ragworms, lugworms, fan worms, and many others

Class Polychaeta

Phylum Annelida

Number of species Almost 10,000

Size 0.04 in (1 mm) to 9.8 ft (3 m) long

Key features Long, slightly flattened body made up of many segments bearing diverse paired, bristly appendages called parapodia; several species bear crown of feeding tentacles; many species are very colorful

Habits Crawling, free-swimming, burrowing, or sedentary tube dwellers; some commensal and parasitic forms are known

Reproduction Mostly sexual; males and females release gametes into the water for external fertilization; mass spawning may be carried out by specialized reproductive individuals called epitokes; ciliated trochophore larvae undergo gradual metamorphosis before attaining adult form

Diet Very varied; may be carnivores, herbivores, or detritus feeders; food is obtained by active hunting, grazing, nonselective deposit feeding, or filter feeding

Habitat Mostly marine and bottom dwelling from tidal zone to deep ocean

Distribution Worldwide

Earthworms

The European common earthworm, *Lumbricus terrestris*, is found wherever there is moisture, including grass, mud, and beneath stones. Length 3.5–12 inches (9–30 cm).

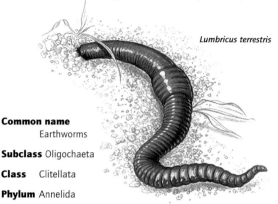

Lumbricus terrestris

Common name
Earthworms

Subclass Oligochaeta

Class Clitellata

Phylum Annelida

Number of species About 3,100

Size From 1 in (2.5 cm) to 13 ft (4 m) long

Key features Long, soft, moist body with annular rings representing body segments; mostly reddish in color, with a few short, stiff hairs sprouting from each segment; in sexually mature adults several segments swell to form the saddle, or clitellum

Habits Mostly soil dwelling or aquatic; use hydraulic action to burrow and swim

Reproduction Asexual by splitting in two (fission) in many aquatic species; sexual reproduction involves mating of hermaphrodite pairs; fertilized eggs are shed into cocoon formed by the clitellum

Diet Mostly plant material

Habitat Soil; fresh water

Distribution Worldwide except Antarctica and arid deserts

Leeches

The medicinal leech, *Hirudo medicinalis*, is the famous blood-letting leech used by doctors over the centuries to relieve patients of all manner of symptoms. Its use was so widespread that the leech almost became extinct in Britain in the 19th century. It is shown above feeding on a three-spined stickleback. Length up to 6 inches (15 cm).

Medicinal leech *(Hirudo medicinalis)*

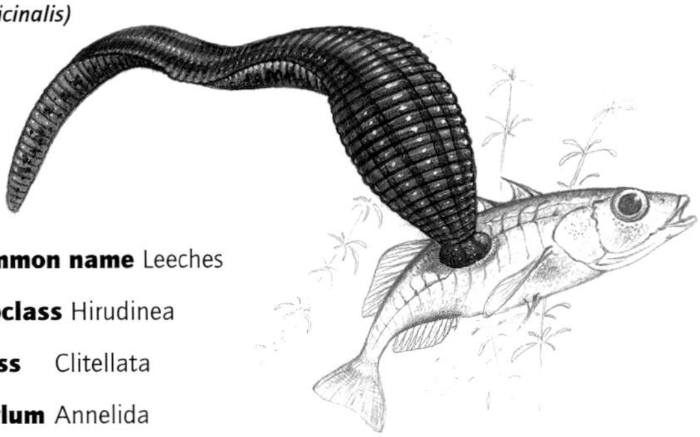

Common name Leeches

Subclass Hirudinea

Class   Clitellata

Phylum Annelida

Number of species About 500

Size   0.4 in (10 mm) to 19 in (50 cm)

Key features Elongated and flattened, with suckers at front and rear ends; body may be bloated after feeding; body lacks externally obvious segmentation and segmental appendages; color variable, often some shade of black, brown, or green

Habits Free living; parasitic on exterior of host; move by "looping" like caterpillars or swim with muscular wavelike contractions of body

Breeding Protandrous hermaphrodites (change sex from male to female); mating occurs; fertilization of eggs is internal following insemination, embryos develop in cocoon secreted by the clitellum; eggs hatch into miniature adults—no larval stage

Diet   Mostly parasitic bloodsuckers; a few species are carnivorous

Habitat Most leeches live in fresh water, but there are some specialized marine forms and a number of species that are able to live on land

Distribution All continents except Antarctica, most common in warm tropical lakes and rivers and on almost all landmasses

CRICKETS AND GRASSHOPPERS
Katydids

Ommatopia pictifolia from Brazil closely resembles a dead leaf. Body length 1 inch (2.5 cm).

Ommatopia pictifolia

Common name Katydids (long-horned grasshoppers) (U.S.), bush crickets (U.K.)

Family Tettigoniidae

Suborder Ensifera

Order Orthoptera

Class/Subphylum Insecta/Hexapoda

Number of species About 5,000 (about 250 U.S.)

Size From about 0.4 in (10 mm) to 5 in (13 cm)

Key features Body form anything from long and slim to short and fat, sometimes with ornamentations on the head and thorax; jumping hind legs tend to be long and slender; forewings (the tegmina) often look like leaves, living or dead; some species lack wings altogether; antennae long and slim, sometimes more than twice the body length; female ovipositor curved and flattened from side to side

Habits Mainly active during the hours of darkness but often seen during the day when they jump into the air and take flight if disturbed; some can be found feeding on flowers during the day

Breeding Males usually attract females by singing; mating takes place at night and is therefore not often seen; females use ovipositors to insert their eggs into plants or the ground

Diet Most feed on plant material, while many will also eat other insects if they can catch them; some katydids are completely predaceous, only feeding on other arthropods

Habitat Among vegetation in meadows, parks, gardens, broad-leaved forests, mountains, deserts, and marshes

Distribution Widespread around the world, with the greatest variety of species in the tropics

Crickets

The black cricket, *Gryllus bimaculatus*, is native to southern Europe. It is bred commercially as lizard food. Being large and stocky it cannot fly, and the male sings a birdlike song day and night. Body length 1–1.2 inches (2.5–3.0 cm).

Black cricket
(*Gryllus bimaculatus*)

Common name Crickets

Family Gryllidae

Suborder Ensifera

Order Orthoptera

Class/Subphylum Insecta/Hexapoda

Number of species About 2,000 (about 100 U.S.)

Size From about 0.06 in (1.5 mm) to 2.3 in (6 cm)

Key features Separated from related insects, such as katydids, by the fact that crickets have only 3 segments in the tarsus of the middle leg, while katydids have 4; jumping hind legs short and fairly stout; antennae long and slim, sometimes more than twice the body length; female ovipositor straight and cylindrical; hearing organ on each front leg

Habits During the day generally found on the ground, sheltering under stones and logs or among vegetation; most are active at night, but some are day active; some males dig burrows

Breeding Males usually attract females by "singing"; mating takes place at night and therefore not often seen; females use ovipositor to insert eggs in the ground, into crevices, and sometimes into plants; females lay just 1 egg at a time

Diet Perhaps the most omnivorous of the Orthoptera, feeding on both plants and other insects; flowers—especially the pollen-rich anthers—a favorite of some species

Habitat Meadows, parks, gardens, forests, mountains, deserts, and caves; also ants' nests

Distribution Widespread around the world

King Crickets

The Stephens Island weta, *Deinacrida rugosa*, is a protected species of giant weta from small offshore islands near New Zealand and occasionally the mainland. Despite its appearance, it is a docile creature—to ward off enemies it simply raises its spiky back legs. Body length 2.4–2.8 inches (6–7 cm). *Stenopelmatus fuscus* is a Jerusalem cricket found in southern and western parts of North America. It is sometimes known as the sand cricket because of its habit of digging in sandy soil. Body length 1.2–2.0 inches (3–5 cm).

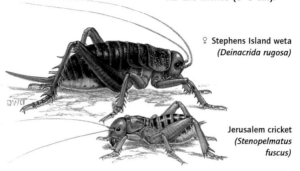

♀ Stephens Island weta
(*Deinacrida rugosa*)

Jerusalem cricket
(*Stenopelmatus fuscus*)

Common name King crickets (Jerusalem crickets, wetas)

Family Stenopelmatidae

Suborder Ensifera

Order Orthoptera

Class/Subphylum Insecta/Hexapoda

Number of species About 190 (about 6 U.S.)

Size From about 0.8 in (20 mm) to 4.3 in (11 cm)

Key features Head large in relation to body, huge in males of some species and often with greatly enlarged jaws; wings absent in all but a few species; eyes wide apart; sound-producing structures absent

Habits Some live in burrows that they dig with front legs; others live under stones or on bark; a few live among vegetation, including in trees

Breeding Males drum against side of burrow to attract females; female may eat the male in some species

Diet Nocturnal scavengers; feed on almost anything, dead or alive, that comes their way

Habitat Rain forest, desert, and dry hillsides

Distribution Worldwide from temperate to tropical regions

Mole Crickets

Male *Gryllotalpa vinae* mole crickets, from southern Europe, stridulate by rubbing their forewings together. Their piercing "song" can be heard hundreds of yards away, making the insect one of the world's noisiest animals. Body length up to 1.2 inches (3 cm).

European
mole cricket
(*Gryllotalpa vinae*)

Common name
Mole crickets

Family Gryllotalpidae

Suborder Ensifera

Order Orthoptera

Class/Subphylum Insecta/Hexapoda

Number of species About 60 (6 U.S.)

Size From about 0.8 in (20 mm) to 1.8 in (4.6 cm)

Key features Fairly short antennae due to living in burrows; pronotum heavily built and oval with smooth outline for moving through soil; front pair of legs highly modified for digging; hind jumping legs shorter than in most Orthoptera; hind wings fully developed; somewhat resemble moles in appearance; both sexes fly

Habits Live in burrows; the drier the soil at the surface, the deeper they dig

Breeding Males sing from their burrows to attract females; eggs laid in female burrow and cared for by female

Diet Plant roots and insect grubs inside the burrows; some species regarded as pests of crops

Habitat Anywhere in the world where moist soil of grassland, fields, and damp heathland is to be found

Distribution Widespread around the world in temperate and tropical regions

Grasshoppers

At rest this European grasshopper, *Oedipoda miniata*, resembles mottled stone. When disturbed, however, it flies off on an erratic course and flashes its brightly colored wings to startle its attacker. *Oedipoda miniata* is found across southern Europe. Body length up to 0.8 inches (20 mm).

Oedipoda miniata

Common name
Grasshoppers (short-horned grasshoppers), locusts

Family Acrididae

Suborder Caelifera

Order Orthoptera

Class/Subphylum Insecta/Hexapoda

Number of species About 7,000 (550 U.S.)

Size From about 0.4 in (10 mm) to about 6 in (15 cm)

Key features Antennae short, sometimes clubbed; wings fully developed in most species although often absent in mountain-dwelling species; hind legs long and powerful for jumping; sound usually produced by rubbing hind legs against the forewings; ears on sides of the abdomen

Habits May be found on the ground, on grasses, low plants, bushes, and trees; some species jump, others fly readily to escape danger; locusts migrate over long distances

Breeding Males attract females with a song; alternatively, they may look for them in a silent, active search followed by visual courtship; females of most species lay their eggs into the ground or at the base of plants

Diet Many different kinds of plants; only a small number feed on grass

Habitat Meadows, parks, gardens, savanna, forests of all kinds, mountains, deserts, marshes, and salt marshes

Distribution Widespread around the world in all but the very coldest regions

Monkey Grasshoppers

Paramastax nigra is a species of monkey grasshopper from South America. Like the rest of the family Eumasticidae, it favors tropical regions. Body length 1.2 inches (3 cm).

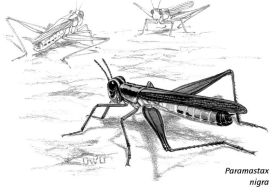

Paramastax nigra

Common name Monkey grasshoppers

Family Eumastacidae

Suborder Caelifera

Order Orthoptera

Class/Subphylum Insecta/Hexapoda

Number of species More than 1,000 (about 6 U.S.)

Size From about 0.4 in (10 mm) to about 1 in (2.5 cm)

Key features Antennae shorter than front femurs; top of the head often projects well above the front of the thorax; often sit with hind legs splayed out to side; females usually thicker bodied and larger than males

Habits Usually found on vegetation, but will descend to the ground to feed on dung

Breeding Like most grasshoppers, females lay eggs in the ground

Diet Dung and plants of many kinds

Habitat By far the majority of species come from tropical rain forests

Distribution Mainly from the tropical regions of the world, but also found in desert and semidesert

Crane Flies

The European species, *Tipula maxima,* is one of the largest crane flies, with wings conspicuously marked with patches of brown. It is a particular favorite of the trout, which will often come to the surface of the pond or lake to feed on these crane flies when they settle on the water in sufficient numbers. Body length up to 1.2 inches (3 cm).

Tipula maxima

Common name
Crane flies (daddy-longlegs)

Family Tipulidae

Suborder Nematocera

Order Diptera

Class/Subphylum Insecta/Hexapoda

Number of species About 14,000 (about 1,600 U.S.)

Size From about 0.3 in (8 mm) to 2 in (5 cm)

Key features Body usually long and slim; long legs; wings may be clear or with smoky patterns; ocelli not present; face often drawn out into a definite snout; larva somewhat caterpillarlike with a definite head

Habits Adults usually sit in the shade during the day, feeding occasionally at suitable flowers; many have the habit of "bobbing" the body up and down when disturbed; larvae live in the soil, in water, or in dead wood

Breeding Males may search actively for females or they may come together in mating swarms; eggs laid in the soil or in water; larvae aquatic or terrestrial

Diet Adults take water and nectar; larvae feed on plants, algae, dead wood, worms, and larvae of other insects

Habitat Forests, meadows, sides of streams and lakes, gardens, mountains, and the coast

Distribution Widespread around the world, especially humid tropical areas

Mosquitoes and Gnats

The ring-legged mosquito, *Culiseta annulata*, can be easily identified by the black-and-white bands on its legs. It is one of the largest mosquitoes, whose bite can be painful, although it probably does not carry any diseases. It is found all over Europe. Body length 0.2 inches (5 mm).

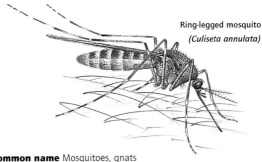

Ring-legged mosquito
(*Culiseta annulata*)

Common name Mosquitoes, gnats

Family Culicidae

Suborder Nematocera

Order Diptera

Class/Subphylum Insecta/Hexapoda

Number of species About 3,000 (over 150 U.S.)

Size From about 0.2 in (5 mm) to around 0.3 in (8 mm)

Key features Slender body, long legs, and rigid, piercing mouthparts (except in the gnats); ocelli not present; males of most species have featherlike antennae

Habits May be diurnal or nocturnal; tend to rest in the shade; blood feeders attracted to host animals by the carbon dioxide they breathe out

Breeding Females whine to attract males; often form mating swarms; females lay their eggs on the surface of water

Diet Male mosquitoes feed on nectar and fruit juices; females feed similarly, but a number are also blood feeders; larvae are aquatic filter feeders or nibble at underwater plant remains and algae; a few feed on other mosquito larvae

Habitat Usually found near water in which they can breed; also forests with plenty of water-filled holes in trees; lake- and pond-side vegetation, marshes, estuaries, human habitations, outhouses, stables, and so on

Distribution Worldwide even into the Arctic

Nonbiting Midges

There are many *Chironomus* species midges, found almost all over the world. The larvae of some *Chironomus* species construct mud tubes in which they live. Adult body length about 0.4 inches (10 mm).

Chironomus sp.

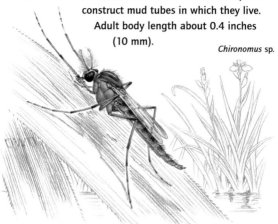

Common name Nonbiting midges

Family Chironomidae

Suborder Nematocera

Order Diptera

Class/Subphylum Insecta/Hexapoda

Number of species 5,000 (about 820 U.S.)

Size From as small as 0.06 in (1.5 mm) to 0.4 in (10 mm)

Key features Resemble mosquitoes, but wings held parallel along body instead of folded over each other; no long, sucking proboscis; ocelli absent; antennae of male very feathery

Habits Unless forming mating swarms, they just sit around on vegetation; at night may be attracted to lights in large numbers

Breeding Form large mating swarms; some species are parthenogenetic (producing offspring in the absence of males)

Diet Adults short-lived and do not feed; larvae feed mainly on plant material, but some are carnivorous, others parasitic

Habitat Almost any habitat except for very dry areas

Distribution Worldwide from the Arctic to the Antarctic (with 2 known species), but absent from very dry regions

Soldier Flies

The larvae of the larger soldier flies such as *Stratiomys* and *Odontomyia* species are carnivorous, feeding on worms, small crustacea, and insects in moist ground. Both species are found in the Northern Hemisphere. Body length of *Stratiomys* sp. 0.5–0.6 inches (13–15 mm); *Odontomyia* sp. 0.3–0.6 inches (7–15 mm).

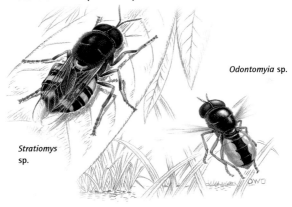

Odontomyia sp.

Stratiomys sp.

Common name Soldier flies

Family Stratiomyidae

Suborder Brachycera

Order Diptera

Class/Subphylum Insecta/Hexapoda

Number of species About 1,500 (250 U.S.)

Size From about 0.3 in (8 mm) to 0.8 in (20 mm)

Key features Thorax may be armed with spines; abdomen rather flattened; often brightly colored or with striped abdomen; at rest wings folded one over the other to cover up the abdomen; males may have holoptic eyes (meeting at the top of the head)

Habits Adults usually found sitting on or under leaves or feeding at flowers

Breeding Not well known, but males of some species form hovering swarms and mate with passing females; may be true for most soldier flies

Diet At least some adults known to be flower feeders; larvae eat decaying plant material, rotting wood, and dung; some aquatic species eat algae

Habitat Forests and watersides; preferably in damper situations, both in the soil and in rotting wood, fresh water, brackish water, and salt marshes

Distribution Widespread fairly uniformly around the world

Horseflies and Deerflies

The 3-spot horsefly, *Tabanus trimaculatus*, is found in the United States and feeds on deer, moose, and domestic livestock. It can also attack humans. Body length 0.5–0.6 inches (13–15 mm). The "blinder" deerfly, *Chrysops caecutiens*, is from Europe. It is called the "blinder" because it bites its host's eyelids, causing them to swell up and reduce the animal's ability to see. Body length 0.5–0.6 inches (13–15 mm).

3-spot horsefly *(Tabanus trimaculatus)*

"Blinder"deerfly *(Chrysops caecutiens)*

Common name Horseflies, deerflies (elephant flies, clegs)

Family Tabanidae

Suborder Brachycera

Order Diptera

Class/Subphylum Insecta/Hexapoda

Number of species Around 3,000 (350 U.S.)

Size From 0.2 in (5 mm) to 1 in (2.5 cm)

Key features Eyes large, usually with brightly colored patterns; body stout; wings often with darker patterning; biting proboscis; eyes of male nearly touching on top of head

Habits Tend to be active on sunny days; usually avoid shade when biting; stealthy flight when approaching hosts to feed

Breeding Males either form individual territories and mate with passing females or gather in swarms

Diet Males feed only at flowers; females take nectar and blood; larvae mainly predaceous, while others feed on decaying vegetable matter

Habitat Wherever the mammals they feed on are found; larvae in water or damp soil

Distribution Worldwide—tropics, temperate zones, and the Arctic

Robber Flies

A robber fly, *Machimus atricapillus*, seizes a lacewing in flight. This species is found in Europe. Body length 0.4 inches (10 mm).

Machimus atricapillus

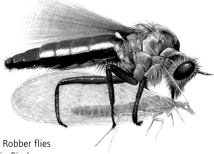

Common name Robber flies (assassin flies)

Family Asilidae

Suborder Brachycera

Order Diptera

Class/Subphylum Insecta/Hexapoda

Number of species About 6,500 (983 U.S.)

Size From about 0.3 in (8 mm) to 1.2 in (3 cm)

Key features Eyes very large in relation to the head, bulging both upward and forward; ocelli present; all of the body, but especially the head, heavily bristled; powerful proboscis; hind legs powerful, used for grasping prey

Habits Adult flies like bright sunshine; sit around on vegetation, rocks, or on the ground waiting for passing insects; mostly strong fliers that catch other insects, especially other flies, in midair; a number of species are good mimics of bees and wasps

Breeding Some species have elaborate courtship rituals; eggs laid on or in the soil, plants, or rotting wood

Diet Adults highly predaceous, sucking the insides out of their insect prey; larvae feed on vegetable matter in soil; some may be carnivorous

Habitat Forests, savanna, grassland, deserts, mountains, and sand dunes

Distribution Worldwide

Bee Flies

The large, or common bee fly, *Bombylius major*, can be found across the Northern Hemisphere. Its long, stilletolike proboscis is perfectly adapted for probing into long-tubed flowers. Body length 0.4–0.5 inches (9–12 mm).

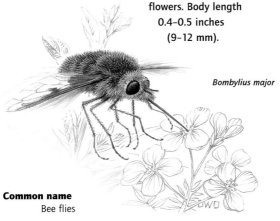

Bombylius major

Common name
Bee flies

Family Bombyliidae

Suborder Brachycera

Order Diptera

Class/Subphylum Insecta/Hexapoda

Number of species 3,000 (800 U.S.)

Size From about 0.06 in (1.5 mm) to 0.8 in (20 mm)

Key features Many rather plump and hairy; may be mistaken for bees, giving them their common name; many have a long, slim proboscis; wings often have darker patterns or spots

Habits May be found feeding at flowers or sitting around on the ground, rocks, or other surfaces; flower feeders may hover as they take nectar; usually seen singly; larvae often found in the nests of solitary bees or wasps

Breeding Courtship occurs in some species, sometimes in leks; after mating, females seek out burrows of their host insects into which to drop their eggs

Diet Adults feed on nectar; larvae parasitic or predaceous, mainly on larval solitary bees and wasps; some feed on egg pods of Orthoptera

Habitat Have a preference for dry habitats such as desert and semidesert, with just a few in more moist conditions

Distribution Worldwide where suitable habitats exist

Dance Flies

In common with other members of the Empididae males of the dance fly *Empis tessellata* present their mate with a gift, usually of a dead insect. However, in the case of *Empis tessellata*, the gift has to be made before mating if the male is to succeed. The species is found in the Northern Hemisphere. Body length 0.35–0.4 inches (9–11 mm).

Empis tessellata

Common name Dance flies

Family Empididae

Suborder Brachycera

Order Diptera

Class/Subphylum Insecta/Hexapoda

Number of species Over 3,000 (725 U.S.)

Size From about 0.1 in (3 mm) to 0.4 in (10 mm)

Key features Bristly flies resembling robber flies but without the bulging eyes; rigid proboscis, which can look overlong for the size of the fly; all have a nick out of each eye

Habits Usually found around fairly dense vegetation, including bushes and trees, or near water

Breeding Complicated courtships involving the male donating a gift to the female

Diet Mainly feed on adults of other Diptera at some time in their lives, but are also avid nectar feeders; larvae mainly predaceous, but a few are vegetable feeders

Habitat Forests and other areas with plenty of vegetation; tend to seek moister habitats

Distribution Worldwide, but at greatest numbers in temperate zones

Hover Flies

Hover flies are common visitors to garden flowers. Many people mistake some of the commonest species for bees. *Milesia crabroniformis* is found in southern Europe and the Mediterranean region. Body length 0.9–1 inches (23–27 mm). The drone fly, *Eristalis tenax*, is an important pollinator, with worldwide distribution. Body length 0.5–0.6 inches (12–15 mm).

Milesia crabroniformis

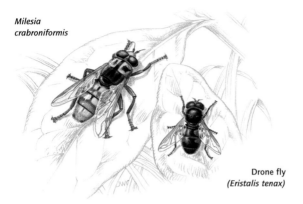

Drone fly
(*Eristalis tenax*)

Common name Hover flies (flower flies)

Family Syrphidae

Suborder Brachycera

Order Diptera

Class/Subphylum Insecta/Hexapoda

Number of species About 6,000 (around 950 U.S.)

Size From about 0.2 in (5 mm) to 1 in (2.5 cm)

Key features Body often striped, mimicking bees or wasps; mouthparts adapted for sucking up nectar; eyes quite large

Habits Sun loving; visit flowers; often form large swarms; usually spend much of their time in hovering flight, sometimes for no obvious reason

Breeding Hovering males attract females, or males may seek out females on foliage and hover over them; eggs laid in various places depending on food requirements of larvae

Diet Adults are nectar feeders; some species also feed on pollen; larvae carnivorous or feed on vegetable matter

Habitat Almost anywhere with flowers from which they can feed

Distribution Worldwide, including the tropics, but at their greatest numbers in temperate zones

Wasp Flies

The Northern Hemisphere wasp fly, *Sicus ferrugineus*, is a common visitor to flower gardens in summer. The female lays her eggs into the abdomen of the bumblebee, using her long ovipositor. Body length 0.35–0.5 inches (9–13 mm).

Sicus ferrugineus

Common name Wasp flies (thick-headed flies)

Family Conopidae

Suborder Brachycera

Order Diptera

Class/Subphylum Insecta/Hexapoda

Number of species 800 (67 U.S.)

Size From about 0.3 in (8 mm) to 0.5 in (13 mm)

Key features Most mimic wasps in coloration and shape; antennae often club shaped; mouthparts of the sucking type, pointing forward; abdomen usually curved downward to some extent

Habits Larvae live in the body of adult bees and wasps, plus a few other types of insect; adults usually found on flowers visited by their host species

Breeding Females chase after bees and wasps in flight in order to lay their eggs on them

Diet Adults take nectar from flowers; larvae feed internally on the host insects

Habitat Sunny, flowery places visited by their bee and wasp hosts

Distribution Worldwide, but with a tendency to avoid the wettest habitats

Large Fruit Flies

Rhagoletis completa, the walnut husk fly, occurs commonly throughout the central United States. The females lay their eggs in the husks of walnuts (*Juglans* sp.) in early fall. Although they do not damage the nut itself, the husks become slimy, and the commercial value of the crop is reduced as a result. Body length 0.2–0.3 inches (5–7 mm).

Walnut husk fly
(Rhagoletis completa)

Common name Large fruit flies

Family Tephritidae

Suborder Brachycera

Order Diptera

Class/Subphylum Insecta/Hexapoda

Number of species 5,000 (280 U.S.)

Size From 0.2 in (5 mm) to 0.4 in (10 mm)

Key features Small to medium size; body often brightly colored; wings with pretty, dark markings; female ovipositor usually visible

Habits Sit on or near the larval food plants; many wave their wings around as they do so

Breeding Courtship varies from none to quite complex behaviors; eggs laid in the host plant

Diet Adults either do not feed, or they take nectar, sap from wounds, or juice from fallen fruit

Habitat Meadows, gardens, forests, marshes, rain forest, and deserts

Distribution Worldwide as long as suitable plant hosts are available

Small Fruit Flies

The fruit fly *Drosophila melanogaster* is found worldwide. It is also the fly species that is probably best known to scientists, who have used it in genetic research for almost a century. Body length about 0.1 inches (3–4 mm).

Drosophila melanogaster

Common name Small fruit flies (vinegar flies, pomace flies)

Family Drosophilidae

Suborder Brachycera

Order Diptera

Class/Subphylum Insecta/Hexapoda

Number of species 2,800 (117 U.S.)

Size From 0.08 in (2 mm) to around 0.3 in (8 mm)

Key features Small, rather plump flies; eyes often red; wings may be patterned; males may have modifications of parts of the body relating to courtship

Habits Adults most likely to be found on decaying fruit or fermenting sap flows on damaged plants

Breeding Courtship often quite complex, with males "singing" to females

Diet Adults take juices from rotting fruit or sap flows; larvae feed on fermentation products, or mine leaves; may be carnivorous or parasitic

Habitat Woodland, rain forest, indoors (especially in breweries, wineries, and canteens); also found on garbage heaps

Distribution Worldwide but more common in warmer parts

Bot and Warble Flies

The common warble fly, *Hypoderma bovis*, is found in the Northern Hemisphere between March and the end of May. It lays its eggs on cattle, which recognize the sound of the fly approaching and attempt evasive action, known as "gadding." These disturbances in feeding can result in decreased yield of milk or meat from the cattle. Body length 0.4–0.6 inches (10–14 mm).

Common warble fly
(*Hypoderma bovis*)

Common name Bot flies (nostril flies), warble flies

Family Oestridae

Suborder Brachycera

Order Diptera

Class/Subphylum Insecta/Hexapoda

Number of species 65 (41 U.S.)

Size From 0.4 in (10 mm) to 1 in (2.5 cm)

Key features Adults heavily built and rather plump; may resemble bees

Habits Adult flies are generally short-lived and stay close to the host animal on which their larvae will feed

Breeding Males of some species defend territories; females lay eggs or deposit live larvae on host; some species use other insects to carry eggs to host

Diet Adults not known to feed; larvae are internal parasites of vertebrates, including humans

Habitat Adults seldom seen; larvae of some species may be seen under the skin of the host

Distribution Worldwide, with a number of species having been spread by humans

Dung Flies

The common yellow dung fly, *Scathophaga stercoraria*, is found worldwide. It was brought to the New World by the first European colonists on their livestock. Body length 0.3–0.4 inches (8–10 mm).

Scathophaga stercoraria

Common name Dung flies

Family Scathophagidae

Suborder Brachycera

Order Diptera

Class/Subphylum Insecta/Hexapoda

Number of species 500 (about 150 U.S.)

Size From 0.2 in (5 mm) to 0.4 in (10 mm)

Key features Rounded head bearing (in predatory species) a well-developed proboscis with "teeth" at the end; often with a rather "furry" body

Habits Dung feeders assemble on or near sources of dung, although adults also visit flowers

Breeding Males known to form groups waiting for females to arrive or to seek out females on vegetation in other species

Diet In some species adults feed on other flies; larvae may be dung or plant feeders (including leaf mining), or predators

Habitat Wherever there are dung-producing animals; otherwise where food plants occur and even the seashore

Distribution North America, Europe, and nontropical Asia, with just a few species in Africa and South America; *Scathophaga stercoraria* found worldwide on cattle dung

Houseflies and Relatives

Musca domestica, the common housefly, breeds in manure, garbage, and rotting vegetable matter. It is found all over the world and can spread diseases and cause food poisoning due to its habit of feeding on both excrement and human food. Body length 0.2–0.3 inches (5–7 mm).

Common housefly (*Musca domestica*)

Common name Houseflies, face flies, stable flies, horn flies

Family Muscidae

Suborder Brachycera

Order Diptera

Class/Subphylum Insecta/Hexapoda

Number of species 4,000 (622 U.S.)

Size From 0.1 in (3 mm) to 0.5 in (13 mm)

Key features Mostly small; differ from other families in lack of certain bristles on thorax; common housefly is a typical muscid

Habits Typically sit around on vegetation or in houses, stables, and other buildings

Breeding Some species court in flight; female lays eggs on or near food

Diet Adults feed on blood, sweat, and plant and fruit juices; larvae feed on decaying plants, dung, and dead animals; can be predators

Habitat Outside in all types of habitat in all types of climate; human habitations, trash heaps, cowsheds, and stables

Distribution Worldwide—many common species have been spread by humans

Parasite Flies

Tachina fera is a common parasite fly found across much of Europe and Asia. It is often seen feeding from nectar on low, flowery vegetation. Body length 0.35–0.6 inches (11–15 mm).

Tachina fera

Common name Parasite flies

Family Tachinidae

Suborder Brachycera

Order Diptera

Class/Subphylum Insecta/Hexapoda

Number of species 8,200 (1,300 U.S.)

Size From 0.1 in (3 mm) to 0.6 in (15 mm)

Key features Body shape varies from robust to elongate, but distinctly bristly; many species resemble the common housefly, while others may be brightly colored; many sit with wings slightly open so that the abdomen is visible

Habits All have larvae parasitic on other arthropods; adults can be seen sitting around on flowers or vegetation close to their hosts, sometimes shadowing host insects in flight

Breeding Males wait for passing females or actively search for them; some species aggregate or swarm; female lays eggs near, on, or within hosts

Diet Adults are nectar feeders; larvae feed on the internal organs of host arthropods

Habitat Anywhere their numerous hosts are found

Distribution Worldwide in virtually all habitats

Blow Flies

Calliphora vomitoria is a very common blow fly, often seen inside houses. Females are known to lay eggs in open wounds, where the larvae grow and feed. On live animals such an infestation is known as myiasis. Body length 0.5 inches (13 mm).

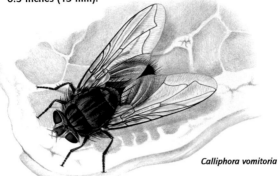

Calliphora vomitoria

Common name Blow flies (bluebottle flies, greenbottle flies)

Family Calliphoridae

Suborder Brachycera

Order Diptera

Class/Subphylum Insecta/Hexapoda

Number of species 1,000 (78 U.S.)

Size From 0.3 in (8 mm) to 0.6 in (15 mm)

Key features Usually shiny, blue, black, or green flies; separated from other fly families by arrangement of bristles on thorax

Habits Often seen on dead and decaying animals where females lay eggs

Breeding Females seek out laying sites by smell and lay large numbers of eggs

Diet Adults take liquid foods such as fruit juices; larvae feed on decaying animals, suck blood, or are parasitic

Habitat Deserts, grasslands, temperate and tropical forests, seashore, human habitations, food-processing plants, and trash heaps

Distribution All regions of the world

Flesh Flies

The common flesh fly, *Sarcophaga carnaria*, is gray-white in color with a striped thorax and checkered abdomen and is found mainly in the Northern Hemisphere. The female fly likes to lay her eggs in slaughtered meat. Body length 0.5 inches (13 mm).

Sarcophaga carnaria

Common name Flesh flies (gray flies)

Family Sarcophagidae

Suborder Brachycera

Order Diptera

Class/Subphylum Insecta/Hexapoda

Number of species 2,000 (327 U.S.)

Size 0.08 in (2 mm) to 0.5 in (13 mm)

Key features Mostly grayish flies; thorax often striped; abdomen often checkered

Habits Adults sit around on flowers, vegetation, tree bark, or near their host insects in the case of parasitic species

Breeding May form groups to feed and court, or males may sit and wait for passing females; females lay batches of eggs on food or single eggs on host insects, depending on species

Diet Adults feed at flowers, mainly on nectar; larvae feed on carrion, dung, or are parasitic on other insects

Habitat All types of forest, grasslands, desert and semidesert

Distribution Worldwide

Water Striders

The common water strider, *Gerris lacustris*, can be found on almost any stretch of still, fresh water. The bugs use their hind two pairs of legs to move across the water, leaving the short front legs free to catch food. Length 0.3 inches (8 mm).

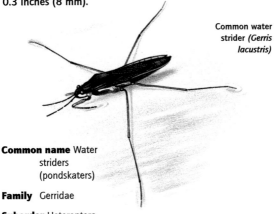

Common water strider (*Gerris lacustris*)

Common name Water striders (pondskaters)

Family Gerridae

Suborder Heteroptera

Order Hemiptera

Class/Subphylum Insecta/Hexapoda

Number of species About 500 (45 U.S.)

Size From about 0.2 in (5 mm) to 0.7 in (18 mm)

Key features Male usually smaller than female; middle and hind legs much longer than body and splayed out sideways for skating on water; middle legs closer to hind legs than to front legs; front legs adapted for grasping prey; body oval to elongate, covered in dense layer of "hairs" that prevent it from becoming wet; wings may be full, partial, or absent; eyes large

Habits Skating around on the surface of water in search of prey

Breeding Once he has found a mate, the male usually stays on the female's back; eggs laid on floating plants or among debris

Diet Small insects that have fallen on the water, small fish, tadpoles; some cannibalism of nymphs is recorded; prey often shared

Habitat All types of freshwater habitat such as ponds, lakes, streams, rivers, canals, and animal water troughs, but excluding very fast-moving water; also the surface of the sea

Distribution Worldwide for freshwater species; some *Halobates* species are oceanic

Ripple Bugs

Velia caprai, the European water cricket, is well adapted to skate across the water with its splayed-out legs and water-repellent feet. It feeds on small invertebrates that fall onto the water and possibly mosquito larvae under the water. Length 0.2–0.3 inches (5–8 mm).

European water cricket
(Velia caprai)

Common name Ripple bugs
(water crickets, small water striders)

Family Veliidae

Suborder Heteroptera

Order Hemiptera

Class/Subphylum Insecta/Hexapoda

Number of species About 420 (35 U.S)

Size From about 0.06 in (1.5 mm) to 5 in (9 mm)

Key features Resemble water striders but in general are smaller and more heavily built; middle and hind legs splayed out for skating on water surface; legs not much longer than body; middle legs halfway between fore- and hind legs; wings long, short, or absent

Habits Found skating around on the surface of water in search of prey

Breeding Females lay eggs among vegetation

Diet Small, drowning insects; small water organisms; mosquito eggs

Habitat All types of freshwater habitat including ponds, lakes, streams (even fast-running), rivers, and canals; water trapped in plants in tropical forests; coastal saltwater pools

Distribution Worldwide, but most common in tropical America and tropical Asia

Water Scorpions

The water stick insect, *Ranatra linearis*, hangs from the surface by its breathing siphon and waits to catch prey such as water fleas with its front legs. It is not a good swimmer and mostly crawls among the weeds. Length (without siphon) 1 inch (2.5 cm).

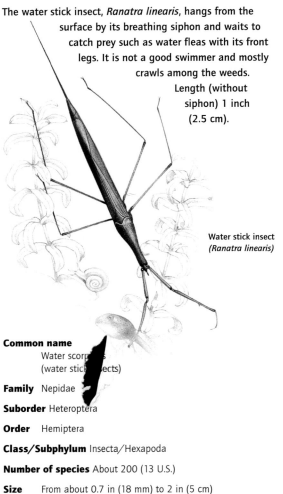

Water stick insect
(*Ranatra linearis*)

Common name
Water scorpions
(water stick insects)

Family Nepidae

Suborder Heteroptera

Order Hemiptera

Class/Subphylum Insecta/Hexapoda

Number of species About 200 (13 U.S.)

Size From about 0.7 in (18 mm) to 2 in (5 cm)

Key features Front legs adapted for grasping prey; body flattened and oval or long and sticklike; fully winged and capable of flight; a long, thin breathing tube extends from the hind end

Habits Walk around on vegetation beneath the water hunting for prey; may hang below surface with breathing tube just above surface, taking in air

Breeding Eggs laid inside aquatic plants; males of some species use their front legs to grasp the female during mating

Diet Insect larvae, tadpoles, and small crustaceans such as water fleas

Habitat Still and slow-moving water of ponds, lakes, canals, and rivers

Distribution Worldwide in suitable habitats, especially in tropical regions

Toad Bugs

The various *Gelastocoris* species of toad bugs from the United States demonstrate clearly the close resemblance of the bug to the real toad, with its large, bulging eyes and "warty" body. However, when still, they are well camouflaged and resemble small stones. Length 0.3–0.4 inches (7–10 mm).

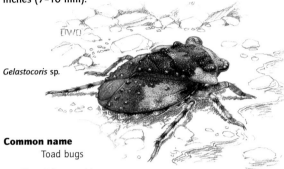

Gelastocoris sp.

Common name
Toad bugs

Family Gelastocoridae

Suborder Heteroptera

Order Hemiptera

Class/Subphylum Insecta/Hexapoda

Number of species About 150 (7 U.S.)

Size From about 0.2 in (5 mm) to 0.5 in (13 mm)

Key features Body oval, short, and squat; rather warty in appearance, like a toad; head quite flat and broad with large, bulging eyes; front legs modified for catching prey; other legs are used to hop along like toads; well camouflaged, usually resembling pebbles

Habits Not very active, but will pounce on any small, suitable prey; adults may swim to avoid danger, but rarely fly

Breeding Eggs are laid into the ground

Diet Mainly small insects

Habitat Along sides of ponds, lakes, and streams; also in decaying wood and under leaves and stones away from water

Distribution Worldwide, but commoner in tropical regions

Backswimmers

The common backswimmer, *Notonecta glauca*, is widespread throughout Europe and lives in ponds, ditches, and canals. It swims upside down, propelled by two long legs that paddle like oars, making it look like a rowboat. Length up to 0.8 inches (20 mm).

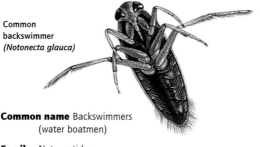

Common
backswimmer
(Notonecta glauca)

Common name Backswimmers
(water boatmen)

Family Notonectidae

Suborder Heteroptera

Order Hemiptera

Class/Subphylum Insecta/Hexapoda

Number of species About 300 (35 U.S.)

Size From about 0.2 in (5 mm) to 0.6 in (15 mm)

Key features Body boat shaped, flat on the underside; usually hang head down from water surface, showing underside; eyes large; ears present in both sexes; rostrum strong and sharp; front legs used to grasp prey; hind legs long, fringed with hairs and used as paddles; wings well developed; underside of abdomen bears water-repellent hairs

Habits All species are strong swimmers, coming to the surface regularly to replenish air supply; also strong fliers, moving from one area of water to another

Breeding In some species males stridulate to attract females; eggs attached to objects in the water, such as stones or plants

Diet Aquatic animals including insect larvae, tadpoles, and small fish as well as insects that have fallen into the water

Habitat Lakes and ponds, water tanks, and animal water troughs

Distribution Worldwide

Plant Bugs

Lygus rugulipennis is a pest of greenhouse cucumber crops. Length approximately 0.2 inches (5–6 mm). *Deraeocoris ruber* feeds on the developing fruit and seeds of numerous plants, as well as on aphids and other small insects. Length 0.2–0.3 inches (6–8 mm). Both species are widespread in the Northern Hemisphere.

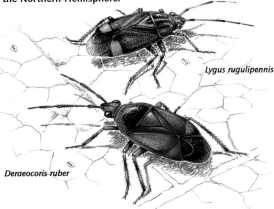

Lygus rugulipennis

Deraeocoris ruber

Common name Plant bugs (leaf bugs, capsid bugs)

Family Miridae

Suborder Heteroptera

Order Hemiptera

Class/Subphylum Insecta/Hexapoda

Number of species About 10,000 (about 1,800 U.S.)

Size From about 0.12 in (3 mm) to 0.6 in (15 mm)

Key features Shape variable; some long and thin, others short, broad, and rather soft bodied; usually fully winged but may have short wings or lack them altogether; often brightly colored, but many species also have cryptic coloration, usually rather shiny; separated from other bug families by having a 4-segmented rostrum, 4-segmented antennae, and by absence of ocelli

Habits Most often found running around on the plant species with which they are associated

Breeding Females insert eggs into the tissues of their food plants or beneath bark

Diet Many species feed on plants and include pests of crops; others are predaceous, feeding on small insects; some species rob spiders' webs

Habitat Found from the ground up to the tops of the highest trees in almost any habitat where suitable plants grow

Distribution Worldwide

Bedbugs

The human bedbug, *Cimex lectularius*, is a notorious worldwide pest. It feeds not only on humans but also on bats, chickens, and other domestic animals. When feeding, it moves slowly over the skin, biting every few steps. It can survive for over a year without a blood meal. Length 0.2–0.3 inches (4–7 mm).

Human bedbug
(*Cimex lectularius*)

Common name
  Bedbugs

Family Cimicidae

Suborder Heteroptera

Order Hemiptera

Class/Subphylum Insecta/Hexapoda

Number of species About 80 (4 U.S.)

Size From about 0.1 in (3 mm) to 0.2 in (5 mm)

Key features Body oval and flattened (appearing more rounded after a blood feed); color yellowish to brown; wingless

Habits All species are parasites on surface of birds and mammals, including humans; active by night, when they come out to feed

Breeding Male bugs penetrate the body of the female and inject sperm into the body fluid; eggs are laid in crevices near the host animal

Diet Blood feeders

Habitat Birds' nests, cellars, and caves inhabited by bats; human habitations

Distribution Worldwide, but mostly in the tropics

Assassin Bugs

An *Acanthaspis* sp. assassin bug feeds on a caterpillar. *Acanthaspis* sp. have been found in West Africa, where they prey on ants. They camouflage themselves by attaching the sucked-out bodies of ants to their back by means of fine hairs and silk threads.
Length 1 inch (2.5 cm).

Assassin bug
(*Acanthaspis* sp.)

Common name
Assassin bugs

Family Reduviidae

Suborder Heteroptera

Order Hemiptera

Class/Subphylum Insecta/Hexapoda

Number of species About 5,000 (106 U.S.)

Size From about 0.3 in (8 mm) to 1.6 in (4 cm)

Key features General shape oval to elongate, some actually resembling small stick insects; short, stout, curved, 3-segmented rostrum that fits in a groove beneath the thorax when not in use; noticeable groove across head behind the eyes; front legs adapted for clasping prey, so they usually walk on the hind 2 pairs; pronotum may have a crest or may bear spikes, which may also occur on top of the head

Habits Walk around on vegetation and on the ground in search of prey, often moving slowly and stealthily; blood-sucking species find their prey by flying in search of it; some species attract prey by using "tools" such as resin

Breeding Females of a number of species exhibit parental care, as do males in some species

Diet Other insects and their larvae; spiders; the blood of vertebrates; one species known to feed on liquid from fermenting dung

Habitat Many species live on vegetation, while others live on the ground or on tree bark; some species inhabit the nests of termites; found in all kinds of habitat—grassland, forests, marshes, and deserts

Distribution Worldwide, but with the greatest variety of species in the tropical regions

Seed Bugs

The small eastern milkweed bug, *Lygaeus kalmii* from the United States, feeds and lays its eggs on milkweed plants. The bug is immune to the toxic chemicals in milkweed but is itself toxic to other insect predators. Length 0.4–0.5 inches (10–13 mm). *Trapezonotus arenarius* is a less common species from the Northern Hemisphere, where it lives on savanna. Length 0.15–0.2 inches (4–5 mm).

Lygaeus kalmii

Trapezonotus arenarius

Common name Seed bugs (ground bugs)

Family Lygaeidae

Suborder Heteroptera

Order Hemiptera

Class/Subphylum Insecta/Hexapoda

Number of species About 3,000 (295 U.S.)

Size From about 0.09 in (2.2 mm) to 0.8 in (20 mm)

Key features Rather tough-bodied bugs, mostly oval in shape; some longer and thinner species; body usually appears flat topped; ocelli present; fully and partially winged as well as wingless forms and species; front femurs enlarged in many species; most are combinations of black and brown; a few are brightly colored

Habits Found either on the plant that produces seeds on which they feed or running around on the ground beneath

Breeding Sound production is involved in courtship in many seed bugs; eggs usually laid on or into food plants

Diet The vast majority are seed feeders; others specialize in insect eggs and larvae; a few are blood suckers

Habitat Forests, grasslands, meadows, gardens, marshes, seashore, and deserts

Distribution Worldwide

Stainers

Pyrrhocoris apterus, commonly known as the fire bug, is found throughout the Northern Hemisphere. It displays the red-and-black coloration that is typical of the family. Large groups can be seen feeding on plants in the spring. Length 0.3–0.4 inches (8–12 mm).

Fire bug
(*Pyrrhocoris apterus*)

Common name Stainers
(cotton-stainers, red bugs, fire bugs)

Family Pyrrhocoridae

Suborder Heteroptera

Order Hemiptera

Class/Subphylum Insecta/Hexapoda

Number of species About 300 (7 U.S)

Size From about 0.3 in (8 mm) to 0.7 in (18 mm)

Key features Resemble seed bugs, but do not have ocelli on the head, and front femurs are never enlarged; also less solidly built than seed bugs and usually brightly colored, often in red and black

Habits Often form large, colorful aggregations on the plants on whose seeds they feed

Breeding Adults produce pheromones to attract one another so that mating can take place; eggs laid on food plants

Diet Nearly all species feed on seeds, fruits, or suck sap from their host plants; a few feed on other insects

Habitat Forests, grassland, deserts, seashore—wherever their particular food plants grow

Distribution Most species are found in warmer climates, mainly in the Old World, with just a few in temperate areas

Bark Bugs

Aradus depressus is a European bark bug that lives under the bark of dead trees, where there is a plentiful supply of fungus to feed on. Most *Aradus* sp.—the largest genus in the family—are from the Northern Hemisphere. Length 0.2–0.3 inches (5–7 mm).

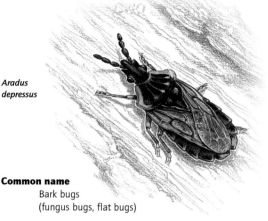

Aradus depressus

Common name
Bark bugs
(fungus bugs, flat bugs)

Family Aradidae

Suborder Heteroptera

Order Hemiptera

Class/Subphylum Insecta/Hexapoda

Number of species About 1,800 (104 U.S.)

Size From about 0.12 in (3 mm) to 0.5 in (13 mm)

Key features Body very flattened, usually oval in outline; legs rather short; antennae short and thick; body often covered in small spines or knobs; also may be pitted so that they are rather "toady" in appearance; usually have camouflage coloration of reddish- or dark brown; some species wingless, others may have fully or partially developed wings; maxillae and mandibles long, thin, and coiled up in special chambers inside the head when not in use

Habits Nearly all live under bark, but a few live on the forest floor in leaf litter or on fungi

Breeding Male lies below female during mating; maternal (and occasional paternal) care has been noted in the family; in species living in temperate climates there is no particular breeding season; nymphs in colder climates hibernate and develop the following spring

Diet All are fungus feeders; a few species feed on tree sap

Habitat Wherever there are trees of a suitable age with loose bark; a number of species recorded among leaf litter in forests

Distribution Worldwide in forested areas

Leaf-Footed Bugs

Narnia inornata is found in Central America. The fat, extended femora complete with spines can be clearly seen. Length approximately 0.6–0.7 inches (15–18 mm).

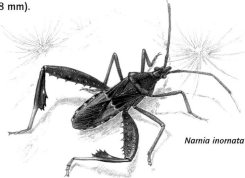

Narnia inornata

Common name Leaf-footed bugs (squash bugs, tip-wilter bugs, flag-footed bugs)

Family Coreidae

Suborder Heteroptera

Order Hemiptera

Class/Subphylum Insecta/Hexapoda

Number of species About 2,000 (120 U.S.)

Size From about 0.2 in (5 mm) to 1.7 in (4.3 cm)

Key features Fairly broad-bodied bugs with the head less than half the width of the pronotum and the fourth antennal segment not curved; membrane of the forewings has many parallel veins running across it; femurs of hind legs often either very swollen or have flattened, leaflike extensions; stink glands present

Habits Usually found on the plant or plants from which they feed

Breeding Males and females may come together as individuals, or they may aggregate in large numbers before mating; eggs laid on host plants

Diet Sap from their host plant or plants

Habitat Forests, grassland, orchards, gardens, deserts, and seashore—wherever their particular food plants grow

Distribution Most species are found in the warmer parts of the world, with just a few occurring in temperate areas

Scentless Plant Bugs

The eastern box elder bug, *Boisea trivittata*, is found on box elder trees in the United States. The eastward spread of the bug is attributed to the planting of box elder trees in parks and gardens. Length 0.5-0.6 inches (13-16 mm). *Rhopalus subrufus* is a scentless plant bug from Europe. Length 0.3-0.4 inches (8-10 mm).

Eastern box elder bug
(*Boisea trivittata*)

Rhopalus subrufus

Common name
Scentless plant bugs

Family Rhopalidae

Suborder Heteroptera

Order Hemiptera

Class/Subphylum Insecta/Hexapoda

Number of species About 150 (36 U.S.)

Size From about 0.2 in (5 mm) to 0.6 in (15 mm)

Key features Similar in appearance to the Coreidae, but in general smaller and do not have thick hind femurs or flattened areas on the hind tibiae; scent glands very small with openings close together, giving them the common name of "scentless" plant bugs

Habits Live on trees, bushes, grasses, and other plants, often with large groups of nymphs together; adults may be found feeding at flowers

Breeding Eggs laid on the surface of leaves, on seed pods, or in bark crevices according to species

Diet All species feed on plants, mainly on young shoots, fruits, and seeds

Habitat Grassland, meadows, scrub, and broad-leaved forests

Distribution Worldwide

Stink Bugs

The bright colors of the shield bug *Catacanthus anchorago* from Asia give a clear indication to would-be predators that the bug contains foul-tasting defensive chemicals and gives off equally unpleasant smells. Length about 0.5 inches (13 mm).

Shield bug *(Catacanthus anchorago)*

Common name Stink bugs (shield bugs)

Family Pentatomidae

Suborder Heteroptera

Order Hemiptera

Class/Subphylum Insecta/Hexapoda

Number of species About 5,000 (222 U.S.)

Size From about 0.2 in (4 mm) to 1 in (2.5 cm)

Key features Broad-bodied, often oval-shaped bugs, nearly as wide as they are long; often rather flattened on top; scutellum is usually triangular, extending over as much as half the abdomen but not overlapping the membranous area of the forewings by much; front of the pronotum may have blunt or pointed projections on either side of the head; stink glands present

Habits Most often found on the plants on which they feed; predaceous species found on any suitable vegetation in search of prey

Breeding In a number of species the females care for their eggs and young; in many species males stridulate to attract females

Diet Many are sap feeders; others feed on insects, especially soft-bodied ones such as larvae

Habitat Meadows, grassland, forests, sand dunes, seashore, marshes, and deserts

Distribution Worldwide, but tropical zones are especially rich in species

Lanternflies

The lanternfly *Phenax variegata* from South America roosts on lichen-covered bark, which it resembles. It often has long filaments of wax protruding from the end of the abdomen. Length up to 1 inch (2.5 cm).

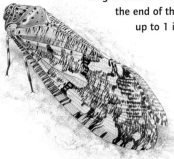

Phenax variegata

Common name
Lanternflies (fulgorid bugs, fulgorid planthoppers)

Family Fulgoridae

Suborder Auchenorrhyncha

Order Hemiptera

Class/Subphylum Insecta/Hexapoda

Number of species About 700 (at least 1 U.S.)

Size From about 0.4 in (10 mm) to 4 in (10 cm)

Key features Both fore- and hind wings covered in a complicated network of veins and cross-veins; many (especially tropical) species have strange growths from the front of the head, sometimes knobbed or spiny; color may be plain browns or greens, or sometimes very colorful

Habits Like most plant feeders, they sit motionless on their host plant to escape detection by predators

Breeding Some species produce sounds during courtship; females of some species lay eggs into the ground

Diet Sap from their host plant species

Habitat Mainly forests

Distribution Usually found in the tropics; a few species in temperate zones

Spittlebugs

The meadow spittlebug, *Philaenus spumarius*, is found in North America and Europe. Shown here are two of the 11 color variations. Length about 0.2 inches (5–6 mm). *Cercopis vulnerata* is from Europe. Length 0.3–0.4 inches (9–11 mm).

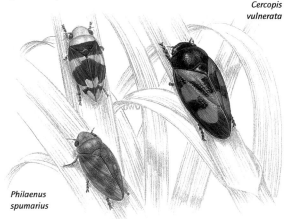

Cercopis vulnerata

Philaenus spumarius

Common name Spittlebugs (froghoppers, cuckoo-spit insects)

Family Cercopidae

Suborder Auchenorrhyncha

Order Hemiptera

Class/Subphylum Insecta/Hexapoda

Number of species About 2,400 (54 U.S.)

Size From about 0.12 in (3 mm) to 0.8 in (20 mm)

Key features Rather squat body shaped like a miniature frog, with powerful hind legs for jumping long distances in relation to body size; either brownish or with bright warning colors; forewings leathery and colored; tibiae cylindrical (unlike the similar-looking leafhoppers, which have tibiae with an angular cross section); nymphs easily recognizable, living in a mass of froth

Habits Normally found sitting on food plants; many adults not noticeable unless they jump

Breeding Females lay eggs in crevices on or near food plants, or directly into soil; some produce protective secretion around eggs

Diet Some adults feed from parts of plants growing above ground, as do many nymphs; others feed from plant roots

Habitat Meadows, gardens, grassland, moors, forests, mountains, and deserts

Distribution Worldwide, with many temperate species

TRUE BUGS
Cicadas

Cicadas are sometimes kept in Asia for their song, as they were in ancient Greece. They are common around the Mediterranean region, where they favor pine trees. *Tibicen plebejus*, a European species, is around 1.2–1.5 inches (3–3.7 cm) in length.

Tibicen plebejus

Common name
Cicadas

Family Cicadidae

Suborder Auchenorrhyncha

Order Hemiptera

Class/Subphylum Insecta/Hexapoda

Number of species About 1,500 (160 U.S.)

Size From about 0.4 in (10 mm) to 4 in (10 cm)

Key features Mainly large insects; both pairs of wings membranous and transparent, held over the body like a tent; males have sound-producing structures beneath the front end of the abdomen; body often green or brown and well camouflaged

Habits Most species live in trees or bushes from which males call to females; nymphs live beneath the ground and are not seen until they emerge to molt into adults; adults fly strongly

Breeding Male cicadas have a distinct "song" to attract females of their own species; females insert eggs into twigs

Diet Adults take sap from the trees on which they live; nymphs take sap from tree roots

Habitat Mainly forests and woodlands; also in deserts where suitable woody plants grow

Distribution Worldwide, but more common in tropical zones

Leafhoppers

The rhododendron leafhopper, *Graphocephala fennahi*, is found in the United States and Europe. Length 0.3–0.4 inches (8–10 mm). *Cicadella viridis* is from the Northern Hemisphere. Length 0.2–0.3 inches (6–8 mm). *Aphrodes bifasciatus* is the smallest of these three leafhoppers and lives in Europe. Length 0.1–0.15 inches (3–4 mm).

Cicadella viridis

Graphocephala fennahi

Aphrodes bifasciatus

Common name Leafhoppers

Family Cicadellidae

Suborder Auchenorrhyncha

Order Hempitera

Class/Subphylum Insecta/Hexapoda

Number of species About 20,000 (2,500 U.S.)

Size From about 0.08 in (2 mm) to 0.8 in (20 mm)

Key features Usually longer and slimmer than the spittlebugs they resemble, with an angular cross section to the tibiae; tibiae bear 1 or more rows of spines; forewings leathery, often brightly colored, distinguishing them from small cicadas

Habits Usually found on their food plants; winged species will readily fly to escape when disturbed

Breeding Many species stridulate to attract mates and during courtship, which may also involve "dance" routines; eggs laid in or on food plants

Diet All species suck sap from plants, often living on just 1 particular plant species; like aphids, they produce honeydew

Habitat Meadows, gardens, grassland, forests, marshes, mountains, and deserts

Distribution Worldwide, but more common in tropical zones

Treehoppers

One species of thorn bug, *Umbonia spinosa*, is found in North and South America. The spiked shape and the green-and-red coloration both serve to deter predators. Length 0.4 inches (10 mm).

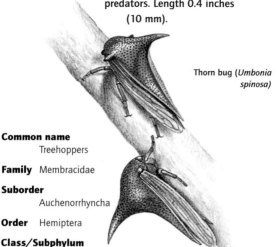

Thorn bug (*Umbonia spinosa*)

Common name
Treehoppers

Family Membracidae

Suborder
Auchenorrhyncha

Order Hemiptera

Class/Subphylum
Insecta/Hexapoda

Number of species About 2,400 (258 U.S.)

Size From about 0.2 in (4 mm) to around 0.6 in (15 mm)

Key features Easily distinguished from the other small sap-sucking bugs by the pronotum, which extends back over the abdomen; pronotum may even extend beyond the end of the abdomen and can assume peculiar shapes, with spines and odd-shaped projections giving a bizarre appearance

Habits Often sit in large groups on their food plants; often camouflaged

Breeding Females of a few species indulge in parental care of eggs and nymphs

Diet Adults and nymphs are sap feeders, releasing honeydew as a by-product

Habitat Forests, grassland, and deserts

Distribution Worldwide, but concentrated in the tropics, especially those of the New World

Jumping Plant Lice

The tiny alder sucker, *Psylla alni*, ranges across the Northern Hemisphere wherever its favorite alder trees are found. Length 0.05–0.1 inches (1.5–3.5 mm).

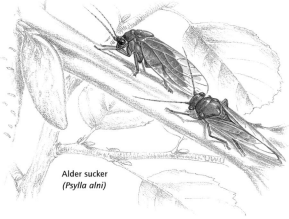

Alder sucker
(*Psylla alni*)

Common name Jumping plant lice

Family Psyllidae

Suborder Sternorrhyncha

Order Hemiptera

Class/Subphylum Insecta/Hexapoda

Number of species About 1,300 (257 U.S.)

Size From about 0.05 in (1.5 mm) to 0.2 in (5 mm)

Key features Resemble tiny cicadas, but forewings more leathery than hind wings; wings held like a tent over the body while at rest; hind legs well developed for jumping, but flight is rather weak; nymphs are rather odd looking, having flattened, circular, or oval bodies with the wing buds sticking out to the sides; nymphs produce waxy secretions that cover and protect them

Habits Adults sit on their food plants, often in fairly large numbers, taking to the air when disturbed; some species make galls

Breeding Both sexes, at least of some species, use sounds during courtship and mating; eggs laid on the food plant

Diet All species suck sap from their host plants; a number of species are pests of cultivated trees

Habitat Most species live on trees and tend to be forest dwellers

Distribution Worldwide

Whiteflies

The greenhouse whitefly, *Trialeurodes vaporariorum*, is a worldwide pest of tomatoes and houseplants. As well as sucking nutrients from the plants, the sugary honeydew excreted gets infested with fungi.
Length 0.1 inches (2 mm).

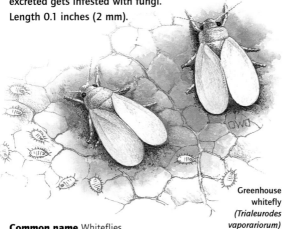

Greenhouse whitefly (*Trialeurodes vaporariorum*)

Common name Whiteflies

Family Aleyrodidae

Suborder Sternorrhyncha

Order Hemiptera

Class/Subphylum Insecta/Hexapoda

Number of species About 1,160 (100 U.S.)

Size Up to 0.1 in (2–2.5 mm)

Key features Tiny insects covered in a waxy powder that gives them a white appearance; membranous wings, which are white or mottled, held almost flat over the body, with slight overlap along the centerline; early nymphs have legs and can move around, later instars cannot use legs and remain in one place

Habits Often found in large numbers on food plants; nymphs cover the underside of leaves; adults fly readily with a weak flight when disturbed

Breeding Reproduction is sexual or by parthenogenesis; when courtship occurs, it can be complex; eggs laid singly or in batches; parental care has been recorded

Diet All species suck sap from host plants; a number are pests of cultivated plants

Habitat Forests, fields, plantations, and orchards

Distribution Worldwide, but more species in the warmer regions

Aphids

Found all over the world, the very common peach-potato aphid, *Myzus persicae*, feeds on more than 200 plants, including peaches and potatoes, on which it is a pest. As a carrier of the fungal disease potato blight, this species helped cause the Irish potato famine in the 1840s, which was responsible for the deaths of almost 1 million people. Length 0.07 inches (2 mm).

Peach-potato aphid
(Myzus persicae)

Common name Aphids

Family Aphididae

Suborder Sternorrhyncha

Order Hemiptera

Class/Subphylum Insecta/Hexapoda

Number of species About 3,800 (1,380 U.S.)

Size From about 0.04 in (1 mm) to 0.2 in (5 mm)

Key features Most commonly green or pink in color, but may be brown or black; females normally wingless; in males both pairs of wings transparent and folded tentlike over the body; body rather soft; abdomen with pair of cornicles on fifth or sixth abdominal segment

Habits Adults and nymphs usually found together in huge numbers on their host plants, on above-ground structures, or on plant roots

Breeding Life cycles can be very complex, including parthenogenesis and alternating of host plant species

Diet All suck the sap of plants, producing honeydew as a by-product; some species produce and live in galls

Habitat Forests, meadows, grassland, moorland, on waterside and floating plants, marshes, and seashore

Distribution Worldwide, but with the greater number of species in temperate regions

Scale Insects

The vine scale, *Parthenolecanium corni*, is a widespread plant pest. It damages the leaves and fruit of the plants it lives on due to the growth of a sooty mold on the honeydew produced by the bug. Length 0.2 inches (6 mm).

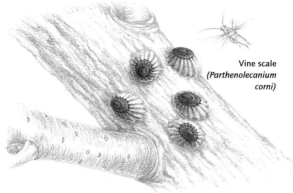

Vine scale
(*Parthenolecanium corni*)

Common name Scale insects
(soft, wax, and tortoise scales)

Family Coccidae

Suborder Sternorrhyncha

Order Hemiptera

Class/Subphylum Insecta/Hexapoda

Number of species About 1,000 (84 U.S.)

Size From about 0.04 in (1 mm) to 0.2 in (5 mm)

Key features Males and females look completely different; males lack mouthparts and have just 1 front pair of transparent, membranous wings, the 2nd pair resembling the halteres of the flies; alternatively, males may be wingless but still recognizable as insects; females may not resemble normal insects: the rostrum is present, but antennae are tiny or nonexistent; normal division of the body into segments not clear; top of the body is covered by a plate resembling a fish scale; wings absent; legs reduced and often nonworking; a powdery or waxy coating may also be present on the body

Habits Females most often found fixed in one place to any part of their host plant or plants, usually in quite large numbers

Breeding Females cannot fly and are sought out by the males; life cycles are quite complicated

Diet Females are sap feeders, often on a single plant species, and produce honeydew as a by-product

Habitat Grassland, forests, gardens, orchards, fields, and deserts

Distribution Worldwide, but more species are found in tropical regions

Mealybugs

Pseudococcus adonidum, also known as the long-tailed mealybug, is found all over the world. It is a common pest of greenhouse and conservatory plants. Length up to 0.2 inches (5 mm).

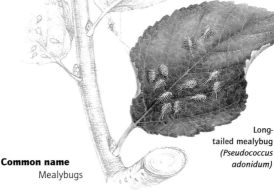

Long-tailed mealybug (*Pseudococcus adonidum*)

Common name
Mealybugs

Family Pseudococcidae

Suborder Sternorrhyncha

Order Hemiptera

Class/Subphylum Insecta/Hexapoda

Number of species About 1,100 (60 U.S.)

Size From around 0.04 in (1 mm) to 0.2 in (5 mm)

Key features Oval-shaped insects with distinct body segments; females wingless; males with a single pair of forewings or wingless; separation of the body into head, thorax, and abdomen not clearly visible in females, but head is obvious in males; males lack compound eyes, but ommatidia are present; whole body covered in a powdery wax coating

Habits With their limited mobility mealybugs are normally found sitting, often in groups, feeding from their host plants

Breeding Females either produce fertilized eggs or live young; in some species females are parthenogenetic, with males not being known to occur

Diet Sap feeders, feeding from either the upper parts or the roots of a range of plants

Habitat Almost any kind of habitat in which their host plants grow, including houses and greenhouses; a number are pests

Distribution Worldwide, but more species in tropical regions

Ground Beetles

The European caterpillar hunter, *Calosoma sycophanta*, lives in gardens and woods. It has been introduced to parts of North America. Length up to 2 inches (5 cm).

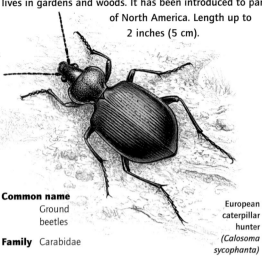

European caterpillar hunter (*Calosoma sycophanta*)

Common name
Ground beetles

Family Carabidae

Suborder Adephaga

Order Coleoptera

Class/Subphylum Insecta/Hexapoda

Number of species About 25,000 (over 3,000 U.S.)

Size From about 0.1 in (3 mm) to 2.4 in (6 cm)

Key features Body mostly black, shiny, and metallic, often with a flush of purple or green iridescence over the ground color; so variable that no one characteristic is "typical"; a small number of brightly colored species; legs mostly long; jaws usually quite prominent; elytra usually with numerous furrows running lengthwise, often also pitted; antennae usually threadlike (sometimes beadlike); eyes usually large; often wingless

Habits Most are nocturnal; during the day usually found under stones, fallen logs, or among moss and fallen leaves, emerging at night to hunt for food

Breeding Mating not usually preceded by any kind of courtship; eggs mostly laid in the ground, sometimes in a special "nest"; adults often relatively long-lived, often 2–3 years, sometimes even 4 years

Diet Many species are predators of worms, snails, caterpillars, and other insects; a few species feed on seeds, fungi, pollen, and other vegetable matter; scavenging for dead insects probably common; larvae may be parasitic on other insect larvae

Habitat Common in gardens and woodlands, less so in more open habitats; many species on the seashore; several eyeless species in caves

Distribution Widespread around the world, except in the polar regions and the driest deserts

Tiger Beetles

Cicindela campestris is a large tiger beetle, with a body length of up to 0.5 inches (13 mm). It is found on sandy heaths and hillsides. The larvae dig burrows in the ground, often near pathways, to catch unwary insects in pitfall traps.

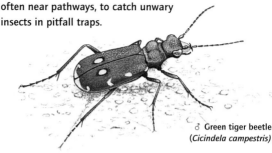

♂ Green tiger beetle (*Cicindela campestris*)

Common name Tiger beetles

Family Cicindelidae

Suborder Adephaga

Order Coleoptera

Class/Subphylum Insecta/Hexapoda

Number of species About 1,600 (119 U.S.)

Size From about 0.4 in (10 mm) to 3 in (8 cm)

Key features Body often brightly colored, metallic, bluish, green, violet, bronze, purple, or orange; sometimes black, whitish, or gray; elytra smooth, widest behind the middle; eyes large and bulging; head wider than that of ground beetle; antennae long and threadlike, inserted above the base of each of the sicklelike mandibles; legs long and slim, adapted for covering the ground at speed in pursuit of prey

Habits Adults mainly ground-dwelling, day-active insects that scurry rapidly around and easily burst into flight; larvae strange, large-headed "s"-shaped creatures that live in burrows in the ground

Breeding Usually no courtship before mating; generally smaller male "rides" on female for considerable periods while grasping her in his jaws; eggs normally laid in the ground, often while the male is still holding the female

Diet Insects, worms, and other small animals

Habitat Mainly in dry, open country such as deserts, salt pans, coastal sand dunes, and heaths; also in forests and along streamsides

Distribution Worldwide, but commonest in warm regions; avoids the very coldest areas

Diving Beetles

The great water beetle, *Dytiscus marginalis*, is found in European ponds and still water with plenty of vegetation. It is a voracious predator, including frogs, newts, and small fish in its diet. Length up to 1.4 inches (3.5 cm).

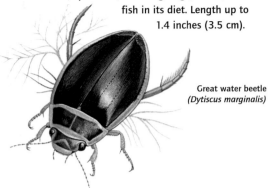

Great water beetle
(*Dytiscus marginalis*)

Common name Diving beetles (water beetles)

Family Dytiscidae

Suborder Adephaga

Order Coleoptera

Class/Subphylum Insecta/Hexapoda

Number of species About 3,000 (about 475 U.S.)

Size Adults 0.06 in (1.5 mm) to 1.8 in (4.5 cm); larvae up to 2.7 in (7 cm)

Key features Adults mostly blackish or brownish with a streamlined elongate-oval shape, convex both at the top and on the underside; hind legs flattened as paddles and fringed with hairs; antennae quite long and threadlike; larvae long and narrow with conspicuous curved jaws

Habits Aquatic beetles that come to the surface to breathe air; both adults and larvae actively hunt prey in daytime; most adults can fly and will migrate in order to find new habitats

Breeding Mating takes place underwater; eggs are attached to underwater plants or laid inside them; larvae may pupate underwater or move to the shore to do so; in areas subject to drought both larvae and adults can survive dry periods by burrowing into mud

Diet Tadpoles, adult frogs, small fish, shrimp, worms, leeches, snails, and water mites; insects such as dragonfly and damselfly larvae; also cannibalistic

Habitat Streams, roadside ditches, ponds, lakes, and pools (including those that are stagnant or temporary); also in hot-water springs and salty pools on the coast

Distribution Worldwide except in the coldest or driest areas

Whirligig Beetles

The whirligig beetle, *Gyrinus minutus* from Europe and North America, lives on the surface film of ponds and slow streams. Adults overwinter in leaf litter near ponds and streams. Short, clubbed antennae are a characteristic of the family. Length up to 0.2 inches (5 mm).

Whirligig beetle
(Gyrinus minutus)

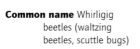

Common name Whirligig beetles (waltzing beetles, scuttle bugs)

Family Gyrinidae

Suborder Adephaga

Order Coleoptera

Class/Subphylum Insecta/Hexapoda

Number of species About 700 (about 50 U.S.)

Size From about 0.1 in (3 mm) to 0.6 in (15 mm)

Key features Shiny-black elongate-oval beetles; the compound eyes are divided into upper and lower sections; antennae are unusually short and clubbed; front legs long and slender, rear legs shorter and paddlelike

Habits Usually seen in groups circling constantly around on the surface of fresh water; adults and larvae are aquatic predators; larvae live below the surface, adults on it; adults usually active in daytime

Breeding Mating takes place in water; eggs are laid in rows or masses on water plants; larvae emerge from the water to pupate on land

Diet Adults mainly eat insects that have fallen onto the water surface; larvae take water snails, mites, and small aquatic insects

Habitat Ponds, lakes, and slow-moving streams

Distribution Worldwide except in the coldest and driest places

Rove Beetles

Emus hirtus, a European species of rove beetle, feeds on insects often found around horse and cow dung. It is only about 0.7 inches (18 mm) long.

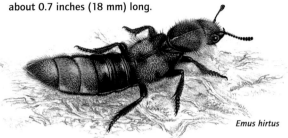

Emus hirtus

Common name Rove beetles (cock-tail beetles)

Family Staphylinidae

Suborder Polyphaga

Order Coleoptera

Class/Subphylum Insecta/Hexapoda

Number of species About 30,000 (about 3,100 U.S.)

Size From about 0.08 in (2 mm) to 1 in (2.5 cm)

Key features Body mostly small, narrow, and elongated; shiny black or brown, sometimes densely hairy, usually with almost parallel sides; elytra usually very short (longer in a few species), often only covering the first few segments of the abdomen; antennae mostly threadlike, sometimes clubbed

Habits Adults tend to run around rapidly with the tip of the abdomen curled upward over the back; many species are nocturnal, although some of the larger kinds are active during the day; most species fly well; some are active in winter

Breeding Many species form aerial mating swarms on warm evenings; eggs are laid in rotting vegetation, dung, or carrion; a few species build "nests" in the ground and look after their babies

Diet Mainly small insects such as fly larvae; also mites, fungi, fungal spores, algae, pollen, diatoms, dung, and carrion of various kinds; some species are parasitic on other insects

Habitat Under damp moss, in flowers, under bark or in rotting vegetation in gardens, meadows, woods, marshes, and mountains (sometimes on the edge of snowfields); more rarely in deserts and caves; some live only inside nests of ants or termites, others inhabit the nests of mammals or birds; many are found on the seashore, sometimes covered by the tide

Distribution Worldwide except in the coldest and driest zones

Soldier Beetles

Cantharis rustica is a Northern Hemisphere soldier beetle. It is usually found on flowers, where it feeds on insects. The beetle is sometimes used by anglers as bait for trout. Body length up to 0.6 inches (15 mm).

Cantharis rustica

Common name Soldier beetles

Family Cantharidae

Suborder Polyphaga

Order Coleoptera

Class/Subphylum Insecta/Hexapoda

Number of species About 5,500 (about 460 U.S.)

Size Mainly in the range 0.4–0.6 in (10-15 mm)

Key features Body mainly black, brown, yellowish, or dull reddish color; often fairly narrow, almost parallel-sided, becoming slightly wider toward the rear end; elytra cover the abdomen only loosely; rather soft body compared with most beetles; antennae mostly long and threadlike, sometimes comblike or sawtoothed; head plainly visible from above; larvae often densely bristly

Habits Adults often conspicuous, feeding in large numbers on flowers or perched on foliage, seldom moving far or fast; larvae mainly carnivorous, rarely seen, living beneath loose bark, under fallen logs, or in damp ground

Breeding Mating takes place in daytime, often on flowers or leaves and may last many hours or even days; males often fight for possession of females, who will sometimes cannibalize their mates during copulation

Diet Adults feed on nectar, pollen, or soft-bodied insects; larvae mainly carnivorous, feeding primarily on soft-bodied helpless prey such as insect eggs, fly maggots, and small caterpillars

Habitat Grasslands, hedgerows, gardens, forests, and mountainsides; rarely in deserts

Distribution Worldwide, but commonest in temperate areas

Fireflies

The wingless, larvalike female of the firefly *Lampyris noctiluca* has light-producing organs that are carried in her last three abdominal segments. This European species of grassland firefly reaches 0.6 inches (15 mm) in length.

♀ *Lampyris noctiluca*

Common name Fireflies (lightning bugs)

Family Lampyridae

Suborder Polyphaga

Order Coleoptera

Class/Subphylum Insecta/Hexapoda

Number of species About 2,000 (about 136 U.S.)

Size From about 0.2 in (5 mm) to about 0.8 in (20 mm)

Key features Body drab brown or blackish; when viewed from above, head is more or less concealed beneath the pronotum, which is also very broad (almost as broad as the elytra); body soft and flattened with sides generally parallel; females often with short wings or wingless and larvalike (larviform); antennae threadlike or often sawtoothed; luminous organ usually present on tip of abdomen

Habits All larvae and most adults are luminescent; light production takes place only during the night; by day the adults rest on foliage and are inconspicuous

Breeding Males fly around flashing their lights at night; the perched females reply with their own lights, acting as a beacon to which the males can easily fly for mating; some species are not luminescent or only weakly so and are active in daytime

Diet The adults of most species apparently do not feed; females of some species attract and feed on males of unrelated species; the larvae are carnivorous, feeding on insect larvae, mites, snails, and slugs

Habitat Mainly in forests; also in grasslands, gardens, riversides, and swamps

Distribution Worldwide, avoiding very cold or dry areas; most abundant in the tropics

Checkered Beetles

The checkered beetle *Thanasimus formicarius* from Europe lives on tree trunks, the larvae feeding on bark beetles. Length up to 0.4 inches (10 mm).

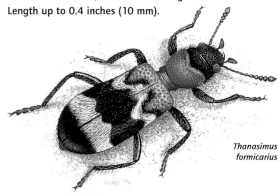

Thanasimus formicarius

Common name Checkered beetles

Family Cleridae

Suborder Polyphaga

Order Coleoptera

Class/Subphylum Insecta/Hexapoda

Number of species About 4,000 (about 260 U.S.)

Size From about 0.1 in (3 mm) to about 0.6 in (15 mm)

Key features Mainly brightly colored beetles, often with checkered elytra; body usually fairly long and narrow, covered with bristly hairs; head prominent, usually as wide or wider than the pronotum, which is much narrower than the elytra; eyes bulging; antennae varied, usually clubbed; also threadlike or sawtoothed

Habits Adults active in daytime, often sitting for long periods on flowers; usually seen singly; larvae mainly live in the galleries of bark beetles or in the nests of bees and wasps

Breeding Mating probably mainly takes place soon after the female has emerged from her pupa; eggs are laid on flowers, in the ground, on trees inhabited by bark beetles, and in plant galls

Diet Adults often feed on nectar and pollen, but also prey on insects such as caterpillars and adult bark beetles; larvae eat bark beetle larvae, the grubs of bees and wasps, or grasshopper egg pods; a handful of species eat stored food products

Habitat Mainly in woodlands; also in meadows, deserts, mountains, gardens, and houses

Distribution Worldwide, but prefer warmer regions; most of the U.S. species occur in the Southwest

Click Beetles

The click beetle *Agriotes ustulatus* has a mechanism on the underside that allows it to quickly jump away from predators. Length up to 0.3 inches (8 mm).

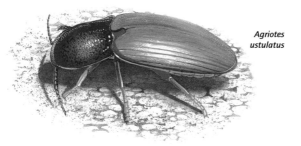

Agriotes ustulatus

Common name Click beetles (skipjacks, wireworms)

Family Elateridae

Suborder Polyphaga

Order Coleoptera

Class/Subphylum Insecta/Hexapoda

Number of species About 10,000 (about 800 U.S.)

Size From about 0.08 in (2 mm) to about 3 in (8 cm)

Key features Body elongate, hard, and flattened, usually more or less parallel sided, sometimes with elytra tapering at tip; mainly black or brown, sometimes brightly colored, often metallic; underside with distinctive "click" mechanism; rear corners of prothorax usually extended into rear-facing points; antennae usually sawtoothed, sometimes comblike

Habits Adults can leap into the air with a distinctive click when laid on their backs; often feed on flowers in daytime; larvae long and narrow (called wireworms), mainly found in the ground or in rotten trees

Breeding Courtship seems to be absent in most species; pectinate antennae in some males indicate pheromones used in mate location; mating is lengthy; eggs generally laid in the soil or in decaying timber

Diet Many adults probably do not feed; others eat pollen, the tender parts of plants such as buds, or small insects; ground-living larvae mainly feed on the roots of plants; others eat items such as rotten wood, small insects, and worms; all larvae feed by external digestion

Habitat Most common in woodlands, but also found in grasslands, gardens, deserts, and on mountainsides; some live underneath stream-side rocks or in the nests of ants and termites

Distribution Almost worldwide, but commonest in the tropics, where some very large and colorful species are found

Jewel Beetles

Females of the jewel beetle *Anthaxia nitidula* are mainly found on flowers, especially yellow ones. The larvae develop under trees and shrubs such as almond and rose. Length up to 0.3 inches (8 mm).

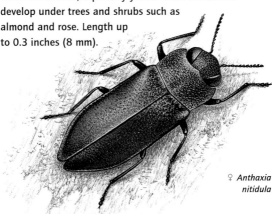

♀ *Anthaxia nitidula*

Common name Jewel beetles (metallic wood-boring beetles, splendor beetles)

Family Buprestidae

Suborder Polyphaga

Order Coleoptera

Class/Subphylum Insecta/Hexapoda

Number of species About 13,000 (about 720 U.S.)

Size From about 0.1 in (3 mm) to about 3 in (8 cm)

Key features Mainly brightly colored, often metallic, sometimes densely hairy; body hard, usually deep and bullet shaped, with a broad head and thorax, tapering off rapidly toward the rear; antennae short, often inconspicuous, usually sawtoothed, also comblike or threadlike

Habits Adults fly rapidly in bright sunshine, bask on leaves or tree trunks, or feed on flowers; females often found on dead and dying trees

Breeding Mating mainly takes place on the dead and dying trees inhabited by the larvae, and in which eggs are generally laid; males may be attracted to females visually or through the release of pheromones

Diet Some adults seldom, if ever, feed; others feed on pollen, nectar, or plant material; larvae mainly feed inside the stems of plants, especially the trunks and branches of trees; some form galls or leaf mines on plants

Habitat Mainly forests, although many spectacular kinds are restricted to deserts and mountains

Distribution Commonest in the tropics, but also found far to the north and south; *Agrilus* is found worldwide and is probably the largest genus of living organisms, with several thousand species

Ladybugs

A seven-spot ladybug, *Coccinella 7-punctata*, in flight revealing its true wings under its hardened and colorful elytra. Length up to 0.3 inches (8 mm).

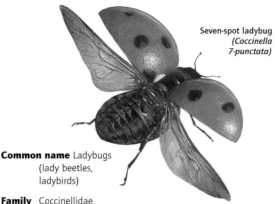

Seven-spot ladybug
(*Coccinella*
7-punctata)

Common name Ladybugs (lady beetles, ladybirds)

Family Coccinellidae

Suborder Polyphaga

Order Coleoptera

Class/Subphylum Insecta/Hexapoda

Number of species About 4,500 (about 400 U.S.)

Size From about 0.04 in (1 mm) to about 0.4 in (10 mm)

Key features Mainly brightly colored red or yellow, usually spotted or blotched with black; distinctive oval or almost round body, noticeably dome shaped on top and flattened beneath; antennae short and weakly clubbed; head hardly visible from above

Habits Mainly active during the day on plants, where adults and larvae of many species are beneficial in eating pests; some species hibernate in huge swarms

Breeding Males usually mate without any courtship; males guard females in some species; females of predatory species lay batches of eggs near aphids; larvae highly mobile and actively move around in quest for prey; pupa (with no appendages visible) attached by rear end to some form of support

Diet Many species feed on aphids; others prefer scale insects, mealybugs, mites, and other soft-bodied invertebrates and their eggs; some species are vegetarian and may damage crops; others graze on molds growing on leaves

Habitat Gardens, fields, orchards, hedgerows, forests, and mountainsides; rarely in deserts

Distribution Worldwide except in the driest and coldest regions; commonest in temperate countries

Fire-Colored Beetles

The cardinal beetle, *Pyrochroa coccinea*, lives around old tree stumps in European forests. The larvae feed under the bark on insects. Length up to 0.6 inches (15 mm).

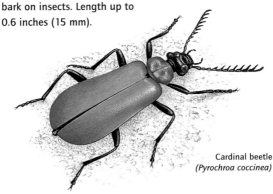

Cardinal beetle
(Pyrochroa coccinea)

Common name Fire-colored beetles (cardinal beetles in Britain)

Family Pyrochroidae

Suborder Polyphaga

Order Coleoptera

Class/Subphylum Insecta/Hexapoda

Number of species About 100 (15 U.S.)

Size From about 0.2 in (5 mm) to about 0.8 in (20 mm)

Key features Elytra mainly red or orange, rather elongate, widening out from front to rear; distinct necklike projection visible behind the head; pronotum narrower than elytra; antennae long, usually sawtoothed, also comblike or feathery; legs long

Habits Adults of some species are often found sitting around on flowers, sometimes on logs; most species are nocturnal and rarely seen; larvae live under bark of dead and dying trees

Breeding Feathery antennae of some males indicate that they probably locate females at night by scent; mating is rarely seen, even in common day-active species; females lay their eggs on dead trees

Diet Adults feed on pollen; larvae feed on other insects beneath dead bark

Habitat Mainly forests; also roadsides with trees, swamps, and scrub

Distribution More or less worldwide; scarce in deserts and grasslands

Blister Beetles

The oil beetle, *Meloe proscarabaeus*, is common in Europe. Larvae creep into flowers, then hitch a ride on foraging bees back to their nest, where they feed on eggs, pollen, and nectar. Length up to 1.2 inches (3 cm).

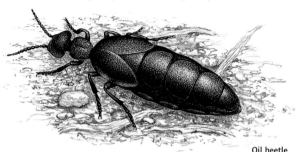

Oil beetle
(*Meloe proscarabaeus*)

Common name Blister beetles

Family Meloidae

Suborder Polyphaga

Order Coleoptera

Class/Subphylum Insecta/Hexapoda

Number of species About 3,000 (about 350 U.S.)

Size From about 0.1 in (3 mm) to about 1.8 in (4.5 cm)

Key features Colors mainly bright, although some species are pure black or brown; body often elongate, sometimes short and fat; head usually broad and connected to the thorax via a narrow "neck"; body often soft and leathery, hard in a few desert species; elytra sometimes short; legs long and slender; antennae threadlike or beadlike

Habits Adults found on flowers, leaves, or on ground on warm days; larvae of many species wait on flowers for a bee, then hitch a ride back to its nest where they will complete development; some larvae live underground

Breeding Mating pairs frequently seen on flowers; some species have quite complex courtship procedures, such as the male striking the female with his front legs or tapping her rear end with his antennae and mouthparts; eggs laid in large batches in the ground

Diet Adults mainly eat leaves and flowers and may harm cultivated crops; larvae live in bees' and wasps' nests eating the stored provisions or in the ground feeding on grasshopper eggs

Habitat Forests, grasslands, gardens, and mountainsides; often common in deserts—most of the North American species are restricted to the Southwest

Distribution Worldwide, but most abundant in warm, dry regions such as deserts and the African savanna grasslands; rarer in dense forests

Darkling Beetles

The cellar or churchyard beetle, *Blaps mucronata*, is often found in cellars and stables. It feeds on vegetable detritus. Length 0.8 inches (20 mm).

Cellar beetle (*Blaps mucronata*)

Common name Darkling beetles

Family Tenebrionidae

Suborder Polyphaga

Order Coleoptera

Class/Subphylum Insecta/Hexapoda

Number of species About 18,000 (about 1,300 U.S.)

Size From about 0.08 in (2 mm) to about 1.4 in (3.5 cm)

Key features Body form variable; color mostly dull brown or black, sometimes black and white or even fairly brightly colored; elytra usually wrinkled or ridged, often fused; eyes almost invariably with a notch in the frontal ridge; antennae threadlike, beadlike, or with a faint club, almost always with 11 segments

Habits Variable; some species diurnal, running around conspicuously in daytime; many are nocturnal or live under logs and stones; others live in nests of termites, mammals, and birds or in stored food products

Breeding In some species the males are horned and fight over access to females; in many desert species males spend much of their time pursuing females over the desert floor; eggs are laid in fungi, rotting wood, and stored products or in the ground; the shiny, cylindrical larvae resemble wireworms

Diet Fungi, grains, field crops, wind-blown detritus, carrion, bat guano, rotten wood

Habitat Most common in deserts (all but 140 of the 1,300 or so species from the U.S. are from the southwestern deserts); also in forests, houses, barns, stables, caves, and animal nests; some species live under seaweeds on the coast

Distribution Worldwide; common in some of the world's driest deserts where few other insects live

Stag Beetles

A pair of male European stag beetles, *Lucanus cervus*, spar for the attention of a female; the stronger one usually wins this pushing and shoving match. Length up to 3 inches (7.5 cm).

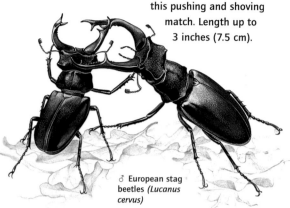

♂ European stag beetles *(Lucanus cervus)*

Common name Stag beetles (pinching bugs)

Family Lucanidae

Suborder Polyphaga

Order Coleoptera

Class/Subphylum Insecta/Hexapoda

Number of species About 1,250 (about 30 U.S.)

Size From about 0.3 in (8 mm) to about 3.5 in (9 cm)

Key features Body mainly large and black, brown, or reddish-brown; sometimes yellow or green, usually shiny; antennae distinctive, elbowed, with a comblike terminal club whose plates cannot be held together (unlike in scarabs); male jaws often large and antlerlike; many species flightless

Habits Adults mainly nocturnal, often flying to lights, sometimes in large numbers

Breeding Males use antlerlike jaws in fights to gain access to females; eggs are laid in cracks in the bark of dead trees or stumps; larvae of larger species take at least 5 years to pupate; it is then a further year before the adults emerge

Diet Adults feed on aphid honeydew and sap leaking from trees; a few feed on flowers; some species probably do not feed as adults; larvae eat wood inside trees

Habitat Mainly woodland; also in gardens, city lots, and city streets that are lined with old trees; absent from areas with no sizable trees

Distribution Worldwide, except in very dry or cold areas

Scarab Beetles

Giant among beetles, male Hercules beetles, *Dynastes hercules*, from Central and South America fight using their horns as pry bars to topple each other over and off tree trunks. Length up to
7 inches (18 cm).

♂ Hercules beetles
(Dynastes hercules)

Common name Scarab beetles

Family Scarabaeidae

Suborder Polyphaga

Order Coleoptera

Class/Subphylum Insecta/Hexapoda

Number of species About 20,500
(about 1,380 U.S.)

Size From about 0.2 in (4 mm) to about 7 in (18 cm)

Key features Body usually stout and heavy, oval or oval-elongate, often brightly colored, especially in the tropics; antennae unique, elbowed, and tipped with a series of flat, elongated leaflike plates (lamellae) that can be separated by opening them up like a fan or closed to form a club; a few species have divided eyes

Habits Enormously varied; some are associated with dung, some with flowers, and others with roots or leaves; many species only active at dusk or after dark, others only in warm sunshine

Breeding Many species have horned males that fight over access to females; some species form "balls" of males scuffling over a single female; male chafers tend to form aerial swarms to attract females; dung-rolling beetles collect dung, others make a "compost" from plant material; many species lay eggs in trees or roots

Diet Larvae feed on dung, leaves, fruit, roots, wood, fungi, carrion, fur, and bones; many adults only eat pollen and nectar

Habitat Almost anywhere; as common in deserts and pastures as in forests or gardens; some species inhabit the nests of mammals, birds, or termites

Distribution More or less throughout the world wherever insect life is possible on dry land

Long-Horned Beetles

A male harlequin beetle, *Acrocinus longimanus*, guards an egg-laying female. This giant species can be found from Mexico to Argentina. Its large body can measure up to 7 inches (18 cm) long.

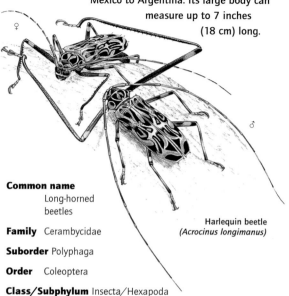

Harlequin beetle
(*Acrocinus longimanus*)

Common name
Long-horned beetles

Family Cerambycidae

Suborder Polyphaga

Order Coleoptera

Class/Subphylum Insecta/Hexapoda

Number of species About 35,000 (about 1,250 U.S.)

Size From about 0.2 in (5 mm) to about 8 in (20 cm)

Key features Variously colored, often brown or black; many black with yellow bands or stripes, some brightly colored, sometimes metallic; antennae normally at least half the length of the body, frequently at least as long as the body and sometimes much longer; antennae generally threadlike, sometimes feathery; eyes usually with a distinct notch; body long and fairly narrow

Habits Many adults active in daytime and found on flowers in bright sunshine; others nocturnal; many nocturnal species are well camouflaged while resting on tree trunks during the day; larvae mostly bore in wood

Breeding Mating often takes place on flowers or diseased trees; courtship usually absent; females may treat males roughly, biting off antennae; males spend long periods "riding" on females until they lay their eggs; eggs usually laid in dead or living trees, sometimes with elaborate preparations by female, such as the "girdling" of living twigs

Diet Adults feed mainly on pollen; some prefer sap or feed on fruit, fungi, or leaves, while others do not feed at all; larvae eat wood or roots

Habitat Mainly forests; also in grasslands, swamps, deserts, and gardens

Distribution Worldwide, but commonest in the tropics

Leaf Beetles

The mint leaf beetle, *Chrysolina menthastri*, feeds on leaves of mint, on which it may be a pest.
Length up to 0.36 inches (9 mm).

Mint leaf beetle
(*Chrysolina menthastri*)

Common name
Leaf beetles

Family Chrysomelidae

Suborder Polyphaga

Order Coleoptera

Class/Subphylum Insecta/Hexapoda

Number of species About 35,000 (about 1,500 U.S.)

Size From about 0.04 in (1 mm) to about 1.4 in (3.5 cm)

Key features Body mainly brightly colored and metallic; mostly rather dome shaped but very variable; some species elongate and resembling beetles of other families such as Cerambycidae; antennae usually relatively short, almost always less than half as long as the body

Habits Mostly active in daytime, usually on living plants; large numbers often occur on suitable host plants, the adults sitting around in large, conspicuous groups; larvae that live in the open may carry "shields" of various materials; many adults can stridulate

Breeding Mating usually occurs without prior courtship; males often ride on backs of females for long periods; eggs usually laid on living plants, sometimes in large, conspicuously colored batches; larvae often feed in dense groups; development from egg to adult is shorter than in most beetles; number of eggs laid can reach 2,500

Diet Leaves, stems, flowers, and roots of living plants; also sometimes fallen leaves; adults often feed on pollen and nectar of flowers; some larvae live inside plant galls or form leaf mines

Habitat Common in all terrestrial habitats; semiaquatic species in lakes and ponds; many species are crop pests

Distribution Worldwide except in the most extreme areas of cold and drought

Weevils

The acorn weevil, *Curculio venosus*, is found in southern England and Europe. Length 0.2–0.4 inches (5–9 mm). *Phytonomus nigrirostris* is from Europe and the U.S., where it is known as the cloverleaf weevil. Length 0.1–0.2 inches (3–4 mm).

Curculio venosus

Common name Weevils (snout beetles)

Family Curculionidae

Suborder Polyphaga

Phytonomus nigrirostris

Order Coleoptera

Class/Subphylum Insecta/Hexapoda

Number of species About 50,000 (about 2,500 U.S.)

Size From about 0.04 in (1 mm) to about 3 in (7.5 cm)

Key features Color very variable: brown, black, yellow, orange, red, blue, purple, green, gold, or silver; body often covered with iridescent scales; some species very hairy; downcurved snout usually well developed, sometimes broad and flat, more often longer (sometimes very long) and slimmer; antennae usually elbowed, tipped by a 3-segmented club; elytra often fused

Habits Adults are usually seen on vegetation; mostly active in daytime; larvae usually live concealed inside roots, stems, or galls

Breeding Male simply mounts female; in some species males conduct ritualistic "fights"; mating is often lengthy, and males often remain with females as "escorts" until egg laying starts; females drill hole in plant with rostrum before laying an egg in the hole; many species restricted to a single host plant; leaf-rolling weevils construct living "leaf cradles"

Diet Adults mainly eat pollen or leaves; larvae usually eat plant tissues within stems, roots, galls, fruits, or seeds; some feed externally on leaves, often in groups; 1 species eats dung, at least 1 other feeds on insect eggs

Habitat Most common in forests, but some prefer open habitats such as grasslands or deserts; larvae of some species live in aquatic plants, others inhabit rodent burrows or ants' nests

Distribution Worldwide except in the coldest and driest areas

Primitive Weevils

An *Arrhenodes minutus* male—found in the U.S.—guards a female while she prepares for egg laying. Length up to 1 inch (2.5 cm).

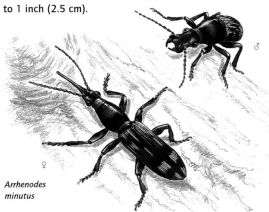

Arrhenodes minutus

Common name Primitive weevils (toothpick weevils)

Family Brentidae

Suborder Polyphaga

Order Coleoptera

Class/Subphylum Insecta/Hexapoda

Number of species About 2,300 (6 U.S.)

Size From about 0.2 in (6 mm) to about 3 in (7 cm)

Key features Body mainly shiny black or dark brown, often with narrow longitudinal cream stripes; distinctive shape, mostly long (sometimes very long) and narrow with sides more or less parallel; prothorax (front part of thorax) shaped like a rather slim pear; snout usually long and narrow, sometimes broader and shorter; antennae usually beadlike, sometimes threadlike; femora of legs swollen

Habits Adults active in daytime on and under bark of trees and stumps; larvae bore in wood

Breeding Males of some species may joust with one another using long lancelike snouts, which are also used to fend off intruding males during mating; female uses long beaklike snout to bore hole in wood in which to lay eggs, often guarded by male

Diet Adults feed on fungi, insects, and sap from wood; larvae eat wood

Habitat On trees in forests of all kinds; some species live in ants' nests

Distribution Widespread, but the overwhelming majority of species are tropical

Swallowtail Butterflies

Queen Alexandra's birdwing, *Ornithoptera alexandrae*, is found to the east of the Owen Stanley Ranges in southeast New Guinea. It is one of seven protected butterfly species on the island. Wingspan 6.6–11 inches (17–28 cm).

Queen Alexandra's birdwing *(Ornithoptera alexandrae)*

Common name
  Swallowtail butterflies (apollos, swordtails, birdwings)

Family Papilionidae

Order Lepidoptera

Class/Subphylum Insecta/Hexapoda

Number of species About 550 (27 U.S.)

Wingspan From about 1.2 in (3 cm) to about 11 in (28 cm)

Key features Mainly large butterflies (including the world's largest), often with hind-wing tails; colors varied, often consisting of just 2 colors, such as black and yellow or black and green, sometimes with red or blue spots; some species (apollos) have semitransparent wings; antennae knobbed but never with hooked tips; all 6 adult legs of equal size; caterpillars often with "Y"-shaped defensive osmeterium

Habits Adults feed on flowers or on salty ground, where they form large aggregations; caterpillars mainly feed singly

Breeding Male and female of most species look very similar; many males use pheromones from androconial scales during courtship; eggs spherical, usually laid singly; caterpillars with smooth skins, often with knobby projections; pupa suspended upright from silken girdle

Diet Adults feed on flowers, damp ground, or dung; caterpillars eat leaves belonging to plants of many families, including poisonous *Aristolochia* vines

Habitat Commonest in tropical rain forest, but found in many temperate habitats such as swamps, parks, and gardens; some species found only on high mountains or open tundra in the far north

Distribution Worldwide, occurring as far north as Alaska

Whites

The orange sulfur, *Colias eurytheme*, is a common North American species. Its favored host plant of alfalfa gives it the alternative common name of the alfalfa butterfly. Wingspan 1.5–2.4 inches (4–6 cm).

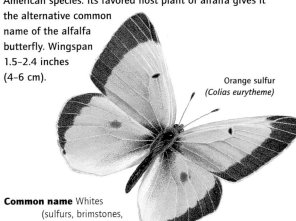

Orange sulfur
(*Colias eurytheme*)

Common name Whites
(sulfurs, brimstones,
orange-tips, Jezebels)

Family Pieridae

Order Lepidoptera

Class/Subphylum Insecta/Hexapoda

Number of species About 1,500 (58 U.S.)

Wingspan From about 0.9 in (23 mm) to about 4 in (10 cm)

Key features Wings mainly with broadly rounded tips; wing color often white or yellow, sometimes with orange or red tips or even (in tropical species) with a brilliant colorful pattern; all 6 legs functional; caterpillar cylindrical, usually smooth and slender, often green; chrysalis supported by both cremaster and silken girdle

Habits Adults spend much time in flight, usually in open, sunny places; males of certain species congregate in large numbers to drink on riverside sand; a few species migratory

Breeding Sexes often look different—males normally brighter; some species with quite complex courtship involving both scent and sight; in most species males patrol in search of females, which often adopt specialized deterring posture

Diet Adults feed on nectar or on urine-soaked ground; caterpillars eat plants of a wide variety of families; some species are widespread pests of cultivated plants

Habitat Mainly open places such as grasslands, deserts, roadsides, gardens, and woodland clearings; many species are specialists on high mountains; numerous brightly colored species in tropical rain forests

Distribution Worldwide except Antarctica

Gossamer-Winged Butterflies

The large blue, *Maculinea arion*, is from Central Asia and Europe. Wingspan 1.6 inches (4 cm). *Strymon martialis*, the martial hairstreak, is from Florida south to the Antilles, and *Lycaena phlaeas*, the American copper, is found across the Northern Hemisphere. Wingspans 0.9–1.1 inches (22–28 mm).

Lycaena phlaeas

Maculinea arion

Strymon martialis

Common name Gossamer-winged butterflies (blues, coppers, hairstreaks)

Family Lycaenidae

Order Lepidoptera

Class/Subphylum Insecta/Hexapoda

Number of species 5,000–6,000 (142 U.S.)

Wingspan From about 0.4 in (10 mm) to 2.8 in (7 cm)

Key features Mostly small and brightly colored; wings usually metallic, often blue, purple, green, or copper in color; often one or more tails on hind wing; male front legs slightly reduced, lacking claws, and with fused tips; female legs normal; face narrow, eyes indented near the antennae; caterpillars sluglike

Habits Adults often found on flowers or basking on plants

Diet Adults feed on flowers or occasionally on sap, dung, carrion, or urine-soaked ground; caterpillars mostly eat green plants; many feed on broods of ants in their nests; some species also eat aphids and other bugs

Breeding Males and females either almost identical or very differently colored; males perch and wait for females; male "blues" patrol in search of females; caterpillars sometimes develop inside ants' nests; pupa squat, oval, usually with silken girdle for attachment; many species have several broods during temperate summer

Habitat In most habitats from deserts and swamps to forests and high mountains; often abundant in grasslands

Distribution Worldwide except in the coldest or driest regions; most abundant in Central and South America

Metalmarks

The lost metalmark, *Calephelis perditalis* from the southern United States and Mexico, is a subtly colored species. Wingspan 0.6–0.9 inches (15–22 mm). *Ancyluris aulestes* from Brazil shows a brilliant flash of red, typical of South American metalmarks. Wingspan 1.6 inches (4 cm).

Ancyluris aulestes

Calephelis perditalis

Common name
  Metalmarks

Family Riodinidae

Order Lepidoptera

Class/Subphylum Insecta/Hexapoda

Number of species About 1,800 (20 U.S.)

Wingspan From about 0.8 in (20 mm) to about 2.5 in (6.4 cm)

Key features Wing shape and color most varied of any butterfly family; mostly brilliant metallic, but sometimes drab brown or with large transparent areas; male foreleg less than half the length of the other legs; antennal club often pointed

Habits Mostly solitary, often puddling on the ground or basking on a leaf; flight usually fast and erratic; most species feed and rest with wings held open; some rest upside down beneath leaves, like certain moths

Diet Adults feed on urine-soaked ground, dung, sap, sticky buds of certain trees, extrafloral nectaries, fermenting fruit, flower nectar, carrion, and human sweat; larvae feed on green leaves, flowers, or on dead fallen leaves

Breeding Males patrol in search of females or wait for them on leaves or flowers, darting out to inspect other passing insects; caterpillars less sluglike than in the Lycaenidae, slightly hairier, and with broader heads; some are associated with ants; pupal shape and color very varied, sometimes occurring in dense masses

Habitat Mostly in tropical rain forest; a few species occur in deserts, grasslands, and roadsides

Distribution Mostly in the tropics of Central and South America; a single species in Europe; a few in North America, Madagascar, Africa, Asia, and Australasia

Brush-Footed Butterflies

The red admiral, *Vanessa atalanta*, is a wide-ranging migratory butterfly that can be found almost anywhere there are flowers and ripe fruit. Adults are particularly fond of overripe and fermenting fruit. Wingspan 1.2 inches (3 cm).

Red admiral
(*Vanessa
atalanta*)

Common name Brush-footed butterflies

Family Nymphalidae

Order Lepidoptera

Class/Subphylum Insecta/Hexapoda

Number of species About 3,000 (125 U.S.)

Wingspan From about 1 in (2.5 cm) to about 3.5 in (9 cm)

Key features Colors bright and varied, often very flamboyant and beautiful; wing shape diverse, sometimes with frilly edges; some species with tailed hind wings; front legs in both sexes reduced to form tiny brushlike appendages, leaving only 4 walking legs; none of the veins at base of wings greatly swollen; caterpillars smooth, hairy, or spiky

Habits Adults usually found on flowers or feeding on damp ground; most species are fast fliers; some species strongly migratory; in temperate regions overwintering may occur in adult stage; caterpillars solitary or gregarious

Diet Adults feed on flower nectar, fruit, fermenting tree sap, animal dung, urine-soaked ground, putrid animal corpses, and human sweat; caterpillars eat green leaves

Breeding Male and female usually look alike, but sometimes look very different; adults often engage in "spiraling" courtship; females may release pheromones to attract males; eggs laid singly or in masses; caterpillars often very spiny, but smooth and green in many tropical species; pupa suspended upside down from its tail, often with silver or gold spots

Habitat In all habitats, but most common in tropical rain forest; many species among the commonest butterflies in gardens, others restricted to high mountain slopes

Distribution Worldwide, occurring north as far as Greenland

Satyrs

The scotch argus, *Erebia aethiops*, ranges from central Europe to Central Asia. The caterpillars hibernate in the second or third instar. Wingspan 1.7 inches (4.2 cm).

Scotch argus
(Erebia aethiops)

Common name
  Satyrs (browns)

Family Satyridae

Order Lepidoptera

Class/Subphylum Insecta/Hexapoda

Number of species About 2,700 (43 U.S.)

Wingspan From about 1 in (2.5 cm) to about 5 in (13 cm)

Key features Colors mainly brown or dull orange, sometimes black and white; some tropical species brightly marked with blue, red, or yellow, or with mainly transparent wings; row of eyespots often present on undersides; forelegs reduced and useless for walking; veins at base of forewings noticeably swollen; caterpillar generally smooth

Habits Flight often rather weak, sometimes rather "hopping" in style, usually near ground, rather than among tree canopy; many tropical species live on or near the ground in the shadiest parts of the rain forest

Breeding Males may patrol, wait for females, or set up territories; females often solicit males for mating purposes by making special flights; male brushes female's antennae with androconial particles; females often drop eggs at random while in flight; pupa generally smooth and squat

Diet Adults of temperate species mainly feed on flowers, sometimes on rotting fruit, decomposing fungi, and carrion; larvae feed mainly on grasses or sedges; a few eat club mosses and true mosses

Habitat In all habitats; temperate species mainly in open habitats such as grasslands, mountain slopes, or arctic tundra; many large species in tropical rain forests

Distribution Worldwide, occurring far to the north in Alaska and Siberia

Morphos

The blue morpho butterfly, *Morpho menelaus*, is found in the rain forests of South and Central America. When the male folds its blue wings, predators are fooled by the bark-colored underside.
Wingspan about
6 inches (15 cm).

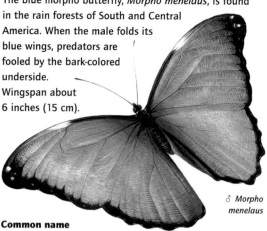

♂ *Morpho menelaus*

Common name
　　Morphos

Family　Morphidae

Order　Lepidoptera

Class/Subphylum Insecta/Hexapoda

Number of species About 50 (none U.S.)

Wingspan From about 3 in (7.5 cm) to about 6 in (15 cm)

Key features Adults very large; underside usually brown with rows of eyespots, upper side often brilliant shining metallic blue; some species shining pearly white, a few brown or blackish; 4 walking legs; caterpillars with conspicuous hair tufts and forked tail

Habits　Adult males generally fly actively around in forest, often following rivers; normally perch with wings closed to reveal underside with eyespots

Breeding Males and females often different colors; males patrol along a beat looking for females; mating seldom seen; dome-shaped eggs are laid singly or in large batches; caterpillars feed singly or in groups

Diet　Adults feed mostly on rotting fruit on the forest floor, but also on leaking tree sap, decaying fungi, carrion, and mud; larvae eat leaves of plants belonging to 6 different families

Habitat Mostly in lowland tropical rain forest, occasionally in drier forest and open, quite dry lower slopes of mountains

Distribution Tropical regions of Central and South America, from Mexico to northern Argentina

Longwings

The gulf fritillary, *Agraulis vanillae*, is from the southern United States and Central and South America. As its name suggests, it can often be seen flying far out over the Gulf of Mexico. Wingspan 2–2.5 inches (5–6 cm).

Gulf fritillary *(Agraulis vanillae)*

Common name Longwings (passion flower butterflies)

Family Heliconiidae

Order Lepidoptera

Class/Subphylum Insecta/Hexapoda

Number of species About 65 (7 U.S.)

Wingspan From about 2.4 in (6 cm) to about 4 in (10 cm)

Key features Forewings usually long and narrow; mostly bluish-black with cream patches, dark brown with red patches (often plus cream), or "tiger-striped" with brown, yellow, and orange; a few species plain orange, one green; 4 walking legs; antennae long; body long and slender; eyes large; "stink clubs" usually present on female abdomen

Habits Adults feed and bask with wings spread; flight is normally low down in the forest understory; roosting aggregations often form in the evening; adults often fly with other members of a particular mimicry ring or mix with them in dry-season aggregations

Breeding Male hovers over female in courtship and showers her with androconial scales; females mate several times and use spermatophores to boost development of eggs; males often congregate on female pupae and try to mate with them

Diet Adults feed on nectar, pollen, urine-soaked ground, and occasionally dung; caterpillars, which are usually spiny, feed mainly on plants of the passion flower family

Habitat Mainly in forests, preferring disturbed, logged, or even felled areas rather than virgin forest; also in plantations, gardens, roadsides, and other more open places

Distribution Mainly in Central and South America, but 7 species as far north as the U.S., of which 3 are breeding residents; 8 species in Asia and Australia

Ithomiids

The tiger *Mechanitis lysimnia* ranges from Mexico into South America, although it is an uncommon species. Wingspan 2.9–3 inches (7.3–7.5 cm).

Mechanitis lysimnia

Common name Ithomiids (tigers, sweet-oils, army-ant butterflies, transparents)

Family Ithomiidae

Order Lepidoptera

Class/Subphylum Insecta/Hexapoda

Number of species About 120 (none U.S.)

Wingspan From about 1 in (2.5 cm) to about 4.7 in (12 cm)

Key features Adult small to medium sized, with 4 walking legs; forewings narrow; wings mostly brown with yellow spots or blackish with large transparent areas; body long and slender; eyes small in relation to thorax; antennae slender, without obvious clubbed ends; hair fringes present along rear edge of male forewing

Habits Adults with slow, rather weak and fluttery style of flight; often form large aggregations with similar-looking species from several families, especially in dry season

Breeding Males may form leks by releasing pheromones from hair fringes to attract males and females; eggs laid singly or in large clusters; larvae usually naked, without spines or hairs, often with fleshy outgrowths along the sides

Diet Adults feed on nectar, fermenting fruit, insect remains, and bird droppings; males feed on withered plants of various kinds; larvae feed on green plants, mainly in the potato family

Habitat Mainly found in the understory of the tropical rain forest

Distribution Tropical forests of Central and South America; a single species in Australia and New Guinea

Milkweed Butterflies

Danaus plexippus, the American monarch, is the only butterfly that migrates annually both northward and southward. It forms spectacular overwintering roosts, the largest being in the mountain forests in the state of Michoacán in Central Mexico. Wingspan 3.5–4 inches (9–10 cm).

American monarch
(Danaus plexippus)

Common name
Milkweed butterflies

Family Danaidae

Order Lepidoptera

Class/Subphylum Insecta/Hexapoda

Number of species About 250 (5 U.S.)

Wingspan From about 2 in (5 cm) to about 6 in (15 cm)

Key features Color range restricted, often brownish-orange spotted with black and white; some pale blue or lemon marked with black; a few lacelike, black and white, others very dark brown, sometimes with blue patches; wings generally broad; antennae without scales; 4 walking legs; larvae have fleshy outgrowths

Habits Adults are powerful fliers and include the most migratory of butterflies; 1 species (the monarch) overwinters in huge aggregations; all species often seen on flowers

Breeding Males generally have large hair pencils that release pheromones during courtship; males procure sexual pheromones by feeding on certain withered plants; eggs are flattened domes with prominent ribs; pupae sometimes covered with gold or silver spots, or may even be mirrorlike

Diet Adults feed on nectar from flowers; caterpillars eat toxic plants, mainly milkweeds and frangipani plants

Habitat In all habitats from deserts to mountains and from gardens to city lots

Distribution Mainly tropical, only reaching northern temperate areas by migrating northward in summer

Skippers

The large skipper, *Ochlodes venata*, is found in Europe and Japan. Wingspan 1.4 inches (3.5 cm). The beautiful long-tailed skipper, *Urbanus proteus* from the southern United States and South America, is considered a pest by farmers and gardeners, who call it the "bean-leaf roller." Wingspan 1.5–2 inches (4–5 cm).

Ochlodes venata

Urbanus proteus

Common name
Skippers

Family Hesperiidae

Order Lepidoptera

Class/Subphylum Insecta/Hexapoda

Number of species About 3,500 (263 U.S.)

Wingspan From 0.8 in (19 mm) to 3.5 in (9 cm)

Key features Body usually plump, hairy, and mothlike; head broad; antennae and eyes set far apart on head; antennae ending in short hook; wings short; color varied—in temperate areas mainly brownish or yellowish, in tropics often beautifully marked with green, scarlet, or blue; some species whitish; hind wings sometimes tailed

Habits Flight rapid and darting, quite unlike any other butterflies; adults often perch with forewings folded flat on each side of the body and hind wings horizontal—a unique habit; a few species active at dusk; at least 1 species nocturnal, all others day-active

Breeding Both sexes may have scent patches on wings, some males have hair pencils on legs; males mainly perch to await females, but some patrol; caterpillar usually smooth, normally with constriction behind neck, often living in rolled-up tube of host plant; pupa smooth, often formed inside a partial silk cocoon within the larval nest

Diet Adults feed on flowers, dung, sap, or muddy ground; caterpillars feed on a wide range of plants, often grasses in temperate species

Habitat In all habitats from deserts and grasslands to mountainsides and rain forests

Distribution Worldwide except in very cold or dry areas, occurring far north into Alaska

Sphinx Moths

Charles Darwin predicted the existence of the Madagascan hawk moth, *Xanthopan morgani praedicta*, before any specimens were ever found. That was because the orchid *Angraecum sesquipedale*, with its long floral spur, had to have a pollinator with an equally long tongue. Wingspan 5.1–5.9 inches (13–15 cm); proboscis 10 inches (25 cm).

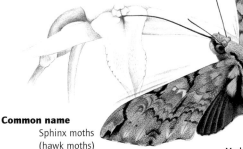

Madagascan hawk moth
(*Xanthopan morgani praedicta*)

Common name
Sphinx moths (hawk moths)

Family Sphingidae

Order Lepidoptera

Class/Subphylum Insecta/Hexapoda

Number of species About 1,000 (about 124 U.S.)

Wingspan From 0.4 in (10 mm) to about 8 in (20 cm)

Key features Body large, heavy, and tapering almost to a point at the rear; forewings long and narrow, much larger than hind wings; forewings and hind wings often different colors (forewings brown, grayish, pinkish, or green; hindwings pink, yellow, black and white, or other bright patterns); antennae thickened; proboscis generally long, sometimes very long; hearing organs absent; caterpillar with hornlike "tail"

Habits Adults fastest fliers of all moths, with very rapid wing beat; most species active at night, adults mostly seen when visiting flowers, with rapid "zoom-hover" style of flight

Breeding Males and females generally look similar, but males are smaller and have a pair of scent brushes on the abdomen; females lay eggs singly while hovering over food plant; caterpillars shiny, wrinkled, and often with stripes or eyespots; pupa often with conspicuous proboscis, normally naked, without cocoon; pupa usually placed in soil

Diet Adults feed on flowers, rotting fruit, fermenting tree sap, or honey; caterpillars eat leaves of living plants; some are pests of crops and cultivated plants

Habitat In all habitats, but most common in tropical rain forests; some species breed in gardens or even on roadside trees in city centers

Distribution Worldwide, but mostly tropical

Giant Silkworm Moths

Attacus edwardsi is one of a small number of atlas moths—the giants of the moth world. Atlas moths come from Asia; however, the population may be under threat because of the interest of collectors. Wingspan up to 12 inches (30 cm).

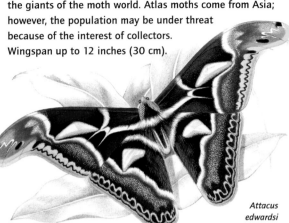

Attacus edwardsi

Common name Giant silkworm moths (royal moths, emperor moths)

Family Saturniidae

Order Lepidoptera

Class/Subphylum Insecta/Hexapoda

Number of species About 1,100 (69 U.S.)

Wingspan From about 1.2 in (3 cm) to about 14 in (36 cm)

Key features Colors varied, often bright and attractive; forewings usually relatively long and narrow, tapering toward tip; hind wings often with spots or tails; wings held out to sides of body when at rest; frenulum absent; head small; body densely hairy; proboscis reduced in size or absent; antennae simple to pectinate in females, usually larger and strongly pectinate in males; hearing organs absent; caterpillar fleshy, usually with bristles or stinging spines

Habits Adults mostly nocturnal; a few species active by day or at dusk; nocturnal species easily attracted to lights; caterpillars may sit in conspicuous groups

Breeding Females release pheromones that can be detected by large feathery antennae of males over great distances; some species conduct visual courtship by day; eggs laid either singly, in small groups, or large masses depending on species

Diet Adults do not feed; caterpillars feed on wide variety of leaves, mainly from trees

Habitat Most common in forests, but also in gardens, city lots, on mountainsides, and open places in general

Distribution Worldwide, but most common in the tropics

Measuringworm Moths

Biston strataria, the oak beauty, is found in Europe and China. Its subtle colors blend in well against an oak tree. Wingspan 2–2.2 inches (5–5.6 cm).

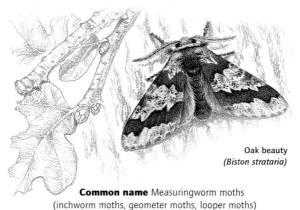

Oak beauty
(Biston strataria)

Common name Measuringworm moths (inchworm moths, geometer moths, looper moths)

Family Geometridae

Order Lepidoptera

Class/Subphylum Insecta/Hexapoda

Number of species About 15,000 (1,404 U.S.)

Wingspan From about 0.4 in (10 mm) to about 3.4 in (8.6 cm)

Key features Color varied: gray, brown, green, or black and white, speckled in various shades or (in tropical species) brilliant metallic colors; body slender; wings relatively large, usually held out at sides when at rest; frenulum present; hearing organ present on abdomen; antennae simple in female, pectinate in male; proboscis may be absent; caterpillar twiglike, with first 2–3 pairs of prolegs missing, giving a looping action when moving

Habits Adults mainly nocturnal, spending the day sitting with wings outspread on leaves, bark, rocks, walls, or fences; adults often fly readily in daytime when disturbed; twiglike caterpillars spend day motionless on the food plant, feeding only at night; they often hang by a silken thread from the food plant

Breeding Males and females generally look identical except where females are short-winged or wingless; eggs laid in batches on food plant; caterpillars generally solitary

Diet Many adults do not feed, others feed on flowers, fermenting sap, dung, salty ground, and fluids leaking from mammals; caterpillars eat a wide variety of plants and in some cases are serious pests of trees

Habitat Found in every kind of habitat but most common in woodlands

Distribution Worldwide wherever suitable food plants are found

Silkworm Moths

The silkworm moth *Bombyx mori* is the best known of the Bombycidae. The species is native only in Asia, but is bred throughout the world for commercial silk production. Wingspan 1.6–2.4 inches (4–6 cm).

Silkworm moth
(*Bombyx mori*)

Common name Silkworm moths

Family Bombycidae

Order Lepidoptera

Class/Subphylum Insecta/Hexapoda

Number of species About 300 (none U.S.)

Wingspan From about 1.2 in (3 cm) to about 2 in (5 cm)

Key features Adult body noticeably large, plump, and furry; wings often triangular in outline, relatively small in comparison to body; antennae doubly pectinate in both sexes; proboscis absent; frenulum greatly reduced in size or absent; caterpillars elongate, with a short horn at the rear end

Habits Adult moths nocturnal; nonfeeding

Breeding Male smaller than female; female releases pheromone to attract male; mating lengthy, lasting 1–2 days; female lays up to 500 eggs; caterpillar pupates in substantial silk cocoon

Diet Adults have no mouthparts and cannot feed; caterpillars feed mainly on plants in the nettle family; domestic silk-moth caterpillars reared on mulberry leaves

Habitat Woodlands, open places, roadsides, gardens, and mountainsides

Distribution Only native in Asia, including India, China, Korea, and Japan

Prominents

The poplar kitten moth, *Furcula bifida*, is found in Europe and Asia, generally flying from April to July. Wingspan 1.4–1.8 inches (3.5–4.5 cm).

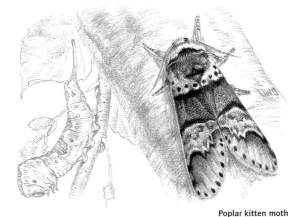

Poplar kitten moth
(*Furcula bifida*)

Common name Prominents

Family Notodontidae

Order Lepidoptera

Class/Subphylum Insecta/Hexapoda

Number of species About 2,600 (136 U.S.)

Wingspan From about 1 in (2.5 cm) to about 3 in (8 cm)

Key features Adult color usually drab, grays and browns predominating, often spotted or streaked with black; toothlike tufts of scales usually protruding from middle of inner edge of forewing; at rest adult holds wings rooflike or rolled tightly around body in a sticklike pose; body stout; proboscis usually well developed; antennae usually pectinate in males and in females of some species; hearing organs present on thorax; larvae variable, hairy or smooth, often weirdly shaped

Habits Adults generally nocturnal; seldom found when inactive in daytime, often coming to lights at night; occasionally found at rest on tree trunks or fence posts; caterpillars found singly or in family groups

Breeding Males generally smaller than females; females release pheromones to attract mates; eggs normally laid in large clusters on leaves of food plant; pupa attached to tree trunks, concealed beneath leaves, or formed in cell below ground

Diet Many adults probably do not feed, others visit flowers or leaking tree sap; caterpillars feed on wide range of plants, especially trees, on which they may be serious forestry pests

Habitat Mainly in forest but found widely in many habitats; some species breed in gardens

Distribution Worldwide in habitable areas

Tiger Moths

The great tiger moth (also known as the garden tiger moth), *Arctia caja*, is found throughout the Northern Hemisphere. Its appearance is so variable that it is rare to find two individuals with the same markings. Wingspan 1.8–2.6 inches (4.5–6.5 cm).

Great tiger moth
(*Arctia caja*)

Common name Tiger moths

Family Arctiidae

Order Lepidoptera

Class/Subphylum Insecta/Hexapoda

Number of species About 10,000 (264 U.S.)

Wingspan From 0.5 in (13 mm) to about 3.2 in (8 cm)

Key features Adults often among the most brightly colored of all moths; may also be white, or drab brown or gray; wing shape very varied, sometimes long and narrow, otherwise relatively broad; proboscis often reduced in size; antennae in male pectinate or simple, always simple in female; hearing organs present on thorax; some species mimic other insects; caterpillars generally very hairy, some known as woolly bears

Habits Adults either nocturnal or day-active (diurnal); diurnal species often very active, feeding and mating by day; may be very prominent in localized colonies

Breeding Courtship very complex; several species form large groups (leks) for mating by day or night; males may inflate large sacs called coremata; some derive pheromones by feeding on certain plants; eggs laid in masses or scattered randomly over vegetation; caterpillars pupate in loose cocoon formed from silk mixed with their own hairs

Diet Adults of many species do not feed; others feed by day or night on flowers; caterpillars feed on lichens or a wide variety of plants

Habitat Found in all habitats from coastal sandhills and saltmarshes to deserts, grasslands, forests, and mountainsides; some species most common in gardens

Distribution Worldwide, but most abundant in the tropics

Owlet Moths

Catocola amatrix, commonly known as the sweetheart underwing, is found in the United States and Canada. Wingspan 2.9–3.7 inches (7.5–9.5 cm).

Sweetheart underwing
(Catocola amatrix)

Common name Owlet moths

Family Noctuidae

Order Lepidoptera

Class/Subphylum Insecta/Hexapoda

Number of species Over 25,000 (2,925 U.S.)

Wingspan From about 0.2 in (5 mm) to about 12 in (30 cm)

Key features Color mostly dull, brownish or grayish; hind wings sometimes brightly colored; some tropical species warningly colored on all wings; wings generally held rooflike over body when at rest; body usually robust; frenulum well developed; antennae slender, threadlike, not pectinate; proboscis normally well developed; hearing organs on either side of thorax; caterpillar generally smooth, but sometimes densely hairy

Habits Adults mainly nocturnal, but some species active by day and night; some species strongly migratory; adults most often found resting on leaves or on tree bark, sometimes on flowers; some adults hibernate; caterpillars can be pests of cultivated plants

Breeding Males may use scent brushes on body or legs to drench females in pheromones; eggs generally have attractive surface ornamentation and may be laid singly or in batches; pupa cylindrical, lying naked in the ground or in a cocoon on the surface; some species pupate in hollow stems

Diet Adults feed on flower nectar, urine-soaked ground, fermenting tree sap, fruits, or the fluids of mammals; caterpillars mainly eat leaves, a number eat decaying organic matter, lichens, or fungi; a tiny minority are predators

Habitat Found in all habitats, the most widely spread of moths; often common in large cities

Distribution Worldwide except in areas of harsh cold or drought

Tussock Moths

Lymantria monacha, the black arches, is common across most of northern and central Europe and is found in parts of Asia and Japan. Wingspan 1.4–2.2 inches (3.5–5.5 cm).

Black arches
(*Lymantria monacha*)

Common name Tussock moths

Family Lymantriidae

Order Lepidoptera

Class/Subphylum Insecta/Hexapoda

Number of species About 2,500 (32 U.S.)

Wingspan From about 0.8 in (20 mm) to about 2.8 in (7 cm)

Key features Adults stout and hairy; wings mostly brownish or grayish; usually drab, but some tropical species brightly colored; some females have only stublike wings; wings generally held tentlike over the back; proboscis reduced in size or absent; antennae conspicuous and doubly pectinate in both male and female, but more so in male; females larger than males; females of some species wingless (sometimes without legs as well) or with poorly developed wings and unable to fly; caterpillars often brightly colored and generally hairy, causing a severe itching rash in humans

Habits Adults short-lived; nocturnal, hiding away during the day and seldom seen; caterpillars mostly found singly on leaves of food plant

Breeding Eggs usually deposited in dense masses, often covered with tufts of hair from the female's abdomen; pupa formed within loose cocoon of silk, often incorporating larval hairs

Diet Adults nonfeeding; caterpillars mostly eat foliage of trees and can be major pests

Habitat Mainly in woodland and forest; some species common in gardens

Distribution Worldwide; commonest in tropical regions of the Old World

Plume Moths

The white plume moth, *Pterophorus pentadactyla* from Europe, is probably the most distinctive of the plume moths, and one of the largest. Its wings are deeply divided into several "fingers," each of which is finely feathered, or plumed. Wingspan 1–1.3 inches (2.5–3.4 cm). *Platyptilia gonodactyla* is found in the Northern Hemisphere. Its wingspan is about the same as the white plume moth.

Platyptilia gonodactyla

Pterophorus pentadactyla

Common name
Plume moths

Family Pterophoridae

Order Lepidoptera

Class/Subphylum Insecta/Hexapoda

Number of species Over 600 (146 U.S.)

Wingspan 0.5 in (13 mm) to 1.6 in (4 cm)

Key features Color usually white or pale brown, sometimes marked with darker brown or black; wings long and narrow; forewings generally deeply notched; hind wings usually deeply divided into 3 feathery plumes; wings rolled around each other at rest and held at right angles to the body, forming a "t"-shape; legs long and slender, usually spiky

Habits Adults found mostly sitting around on leaves or flowers; flight weak and fluttering; most species nocturnal, but some active by day

Breeding Females lay eggs in plants; larvae mainly live externally on plants; some live within rolled leaves or bore into plant tissues; pupa may be suspended by silken cremaster or lie on the ground, protected by a cocoon

Diet Adults feed on flowers; caterpillars eat plants of many families, especially the daisy family

Habitat Found in all habitats from coastal salt marshes to mountainsides, deserts, forests, and backyards

Distribution Worldwide except in regions with extreme or harsh climates

Clearwinged Moths

The hornet moth, *Sesia apiformis*, ranges throughout most of Europe, except for the northernmost areas. Its yellow-and-brown striped body makes it an excellent wasp mimic. Wingspan 1.4–1.8 inches (3.5–4.5 cm).

Hornet moth
(Sesia apiformis)

Common name Clearwinged moths (borer moths)

Family Sesiidae

Order Lepidoptera

Class/Subphylum Insecta/Hexapoda

Number of species About 800 (115 U.S.)

Wingspan From about 0.5 in (13 mm) to about 2.4 in (6 cm)

Key features Adult often wasplike, frequently banded in black and yellow or black and red; wings distinctive, with large areas transparent and bare of scales; forewings much narrower than hind wings; wings held partly open at rest, exposing pattern on abdomen; fringes of hair on legs, which may have shaggy appearance; antennae tapering at both ends, simple or comblike, often with tuft of bristles at tip

Habits Adults active by day, usually in bright sunshine; in flight resemblance to wasps is often very strong; adults feed on flowers or rest on leaves

Breeding Females sit on leaves and expand anal tuft of hair, releasing pheromones to attract males; mating takes place back to back, usually in daytime on food plant; females lay eggs on stems of plants in which larvae bore feeding tunnels

Diet Adults feed at flowers; larvae bore into the roots and stems of various plants, especially shrubs

Habitat In all habitats, especially woodlands; also grasslands, mountainsides, and gardens

Distribution Worldwide, but most abundant in the tropics of Africa and Asia

Bagworm Moths

Canephora unicolor is the largest of the 200 or so species of bagworm found in Europe. The bag is constructed from natural materials collected by the caterpillar. The adult female never leaves the bag. Wingspan 1 inch (2.5 cm).

Canephora unicolor

Common name
Bagworm moths

Family Psychidae

Order Lepidoptera

Class/Subphylum Insecta/Hexapoda

Number of species About 800 (26 U.S.)

Wingspan From about 0.6 in (15 mm) to about 1.4 in (3.5 cm)

Key features Adults mainly drab, usually brownish; some tropical species are more colorful; wings occasionally almost scaleless and transparent; body hairy; mouthparts reduced and nonfunctional; females frequently wingless; caterpillars live inside bag composed of silk mixed with various natural materials

Habits Bagworm adults only very rarely seen; bags made by caterpillars may be conspicuous on various plants

Breeding Marked differences in most species between males and females; females wingless and remain inside bag in which they mate and lay their eggs; males fully winged and fly to find females; caterpillars pupate within bag

Diet Adults do not feed; caterpillars eat wide variety of plants; some can be serious pests of cultivated plants

Habitat In most habitats, but prefer forested areas

Distribution Worldwide, but far more common in the tropics than elsewhere

Ermine Moths

The Ailanthus webworm moth, *Atteva punctella* from Central and South America and the United States, seen in a typical pose with its wings tightly wrapped around its body. Wingspan 0.7–1.2 inches (18–30 mm.)

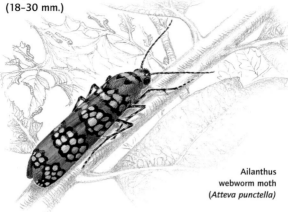

Ailanthus
webworm moth
(*Atteva punctella*)

Common name Ermine moths

Family Yponomeutidae

Order Lepidoptera

Class/Subphylum Insecta/Hexapoda

Number of species About 800 (32 U.S.)

Wingspan From about 0.5 in (13 mm) to about 1.2 in (3 cm)

Key features Wing pattern sometimes colorful, but often white peppered with black dots; body and wings quite long and narrow; wings wrapped closely around body at rest, giving torpedolike outline; wing tips blunt; antennae directed straight out in front of head, like horns; head covered with scales

Habits Adults generally rest on food plants by day; larvae often live in extensive silken webbing slung across their food plant or sometimes live as miners within leaves (larvae of different generations may attack different parts of the host plant); larvae generally gregarious, sometimes solitary; pupae often hung in large clusters within webbing

Breeding Male and female both release sexual pheromones; some species produce 3 generations per year; larva constructs cocoon in which to pupate

Diet Adults do not feed; larvae eat wide variety of plants

Habitat In all habitats; some species are major pests of agriculture

Distribution Almost worldwide; most common in the tropics

Sawflies and Allies

The European giant horntail, *Urocerus gigas*, is a pest of spruce trees—the larvae live in the heartwood and transmit a fungus that may eventually kill the trees. Body length 1.4 inches (3.5 cm).

Giant horntail
(*Urocerus gigas*)

Common name Sawflies, wood wasps (horntails)

Suborder Symphyta

Order Hymenoptera

Class/Subphylum Insecta/Hexapoda

Number of species About 10,000 (about 1,000 U.S.)

Size From about 0.1 in (3 mm) to about 1.2 in (3 cm)

Key features Color variable, frequently black, often with yellow or red stripes or bands; also green or metallic bluish; abdomen broadly attached to thorax with no "waist"; wing venation complex; antennae variable, may be featherlike in males; female has sawlike ovipositor; larvae mostly caterpillarlike

Habits Adults mostly weak fliers and active during the day; often seen on flowers, leaves, or the trunks of trees; larvae mostly found in groups on leaves

Breeding Males and females find one another by pheromones or visually; mating usually takes place in back-to-back position; females lay eggs in leaves using sawlike ovipositor or in timber using longer, screwlike ovipositor

Diet Adults feed on nectar, other insects, or not at all; larvae mostly feed on leaves or wood, but a few are predatory; some species form galls on plants

Habitat Mostly woodlands, some species also in grasslands and mountainsides; a few species may be pests in gardens, orchards, and on field crops

Distribution Mainly in cool temperate regions and in Australia; much scarcer in the tropics

Ichneumon Wasps

Gasteruption jaculator (family Gasteruptiidae) has the common name of banner wasp and is found in northern and central Europe. Like many species of parasitic wasps, its larvae feed on the larvae of solitary bees. Body length 0.6 inches (15 mm).

Banner wasp
(*Gasteruption jaculator*)

Common name Ichneumon wasps

Family Ichneumonidae

Division Parasitica

Suborder Apocrita

Order Hymenoptera

Class/Subphylum Insecta/Hexapoda

Number of species About 60,000 (about 12,000 U.S.)

Size From about 0.1 in (3 mm) to about 3 in (7.5 cm)

Key features Body often long and slender, usually black, often with red, white, or yellow markings; female may have long needlelike ovipositor; long, constantly moving antennae with 13 or more segments, often tipped white; adults usually fully winged, but occasionally with shortened wings or none at all

Habits Adults often found on flowers or walking across foliage searching for hosts; larvae are parasites on other invertebrates, mainly insects

Breeding Little is known about mating habits in most species; in some species mating occurs on the tree trunks from which the adults emerged; females seek out hosts such as caterpillars in which to lay eggs; certain species can penetrate solid bark to lay eggs in larvae burrowing within; ichneumon larvae consume their living host, eventually killing it

Diet Adults feed on nectar, aphid honeydew, or liquids leaking from host, often from punctures made by the ovipositor; larvae feed parasitically on living invertebrates, especially caterpillars of Lepidoptera; a few feed on plant products stored by host

Habitat In all terrestrial habitats; most common in temperate forests and grassland, rare in arid zones

Distribution Worldwide except in very dry or cold areas

Gall Wasps

Diplolepis rosae, the European gall wasp, makes a "robin pincushion" gall on the wild rose.
Body length 0.2 inches (5 mm).

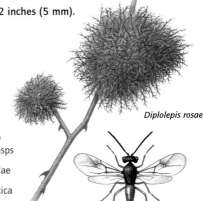

Diplolepis rosae

Common name
Gall wasps

Family Cynipidae

Division Parasitica

Suborder Apocrita

Order Hymenoptera

Class/Subphylum Insecta/Hexapoda

Number of species Over 2,000 (over 200 U.S.)

Size From about 0.08 in (2 mm) to about 0.3 in (8 mm)

Key features Body black or dark brown, glossy, with humpbacked profile; abdomen of female flattened from side to side; wings with only a small number of veins; some species wingless; antennae long with 13 or 14 segments in females, 14 or 15 in males

Habits Adults small, secretive, and seldom seen; larvae form galls, which can be highly conspicuous on plants

Breeding Females lay eggs in plant tissues, usually restricting their attacks to just a single species of host plant; the plant responds by forming a gall in which the larvae feed

Diet Adults feed on nectar or honeydew or not at all; larvae mostly feed on plants, a few on other insects

Habitat Common in all terrestrial habitats, including deserts, from ground level to the tops of trees

Distribution Worldwide, but they avoid the driest and coldest zones

Cuckoo Wasps

The larvae of *Chrysis fuscipennis* from the Northern Hemisphere live in the nests of potter wasps (Vespidae), feeding on the egg, larva, and any stored food of their host. Adult body length 0.4 inches (10 mm).

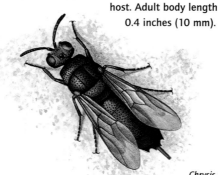

Chrysis fuscipennis

Common name
Cuckoo wasps
(jewel wasps, ruby-tailed wasps)

Family Chrysididae

Suborder Apocrita

Order Hymenoptera

Class/Subphylum Insecta/Hexapoda

Number of species About 3,000 (about 130 U.S.)

Size From about 0.1 in (3 mm) to about 0.5 in (13 mm)

Key features Body hard, metallic, usually brightly colored, often green or red and green, but sometimes with a blue or golden shimmer; thorax armored, usually densely covered in small pits; only 3 abdominal segments visible from above; underside of abdomen flat or concave; sting usually nonfunctional; males and females difficult to distinguish

Habits Active in bright sunshine near the nests of their host bees and wasps; usually seen running on gate posts, fences, tree trunks, walls, rock faces, or bare ground

Breeding Most species lay eggs in nests of bees or wasps; the cuckoo wasp larva eats the host larva and its stock of food; some species parasitic on other types of insects such as bugs

Diet Adults feed on nectar and honeydew; larvae feed on broods of bees and wasps and their stored food

Habitat Woods, meadows, deserts, mountains, disused lots, and gardens

Distribution Worldwide, but commoner in warmer zones

Digger Wasps

The largest of the European hymenopterans, the yellow-faced digger wasp, *Scolia flavifrons* from southern Europe, is harmless to humans. However, it is a parasite on the beetle *Oryctes nasicornis*. Body length 1.6 inches (4 cm).

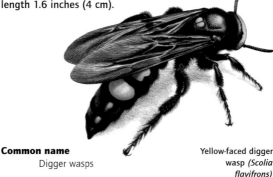

Yellow-faced digger wasp *(Scolia flavifrons)*

Common name
　Digger wasps

Family　Scoliidae

Suborder　Apocrita

Order　Hymenoptera

Class/Subphylum　Insecta/Hexapoda

Number of species　About 300 (about 20 U.S.)

Size　From about 0.5 in (13 mm) to about 2.4 in (6 cm)

Key features　Mostly large, robustly built, hairy wasps; color usually black marked with brown, orange, or yellow; both sexes fully winged; female antennae 12-segmented, male antennae 13-segmented; outer sections of forewings have a corrugated appearance

Habits　Adults mainly found on flowers in bright sunshine; larvae live underground on beetle larvae

Breeding　Males considerably smaller and slimmer than females; males and females perform a "mating dance"; female digs into ground and lays egg on large beetle larvae

Diet　Adults feed on flower nectar; larvae feed on living beetle larvae

Habitat　Open countryside, meadows, mountainsides, coastal sand dunes, gardens, and woodland edges

Distribution　Mainly in warmer parts of world; in North America as far north as southern Canada

Velvet Ants

The European velvet ant, *Mutilla europaea*, is a parasite whose larvae develop inside bumblebee nests. The females can be found running around on the ground, in leaf litter, or on tree trunks with an agitated, antlike gait. Body length 0.5 inches (13 mm).

Mutilla europaea

Common name
Velvet ants

Family Mutillidae

Suborder Apocrita

Order Hymenoptera

Class/Subphylum Insecta/Hexapoda

Number of species About 5,000 (about 450 U.S.)

Size From about 0.2 in (5 mm) to about 1 in (2.5 cm)

Key features Body more sturdily built than in real ants (Formicidae), with less of a "waist"; densely covered in hair, usually brightly colored, often black and white or black and orange; females wingless, males fully winged; unlike ants, antennae are not elbowed; female has powerful sting

Habits Females usually seen running on open ground, less often across vegetation or up tree trunks; males usually found feeding on flowers

Breeding Males are often much larger than the wingless females and carry them off in a mating flight; females search for nests of bees and wasps in which to lay their eggs

Diet Adults normally feed on nectar, but females may attack other bees and wasps for food; larvae feed on larvae and pupae of bees, wasps, and flies

Habitat Most often found running on the ground in open, dry places such as deserts; in the U.S. most species restricted to the arid zones of the Southwest; also found in rain forests, meadows, and on mountains

Distribution Worldwide, but uncommon in cooler temperate zones

Ants

Solenopsis geminata, the North American fire ant, is a serious crop pest. The common name derives from the burning sensation caused by the ants' venomous bites. Body length 0.03–0.2 inches (1–6 mm).

Fire ant
(*Solenopsis geminata*)

Common name Ants

Family Formicidae

Suborder Apocrita

Order Hymenoptera

Class/Subphylum Insecta/Hexapoda

Number of species About 15,000 (about 600 U.S.)

Size From about 0.04 in (1 mm) to about 1.4 in (3.5 cm)

Key features Body usually black, brown, reddish, or yellowish; eyes small; antennae elbowed; waist (known as a pedicel) with one or two beadlike or scalelike segments; stinger may be present; wings absent in workers—usually present in sexual forms, but discarded later

Habits All ants are fully social, often constructing very large nests containing thousands of individuals; some species live in the nests of others or take other species as slaves

Breeding Most species release large numbers of winged males and females, which form nuptial swarms; after mating, queens break off their wings and establish new nest, usually without help of male, who normally dies (unlike in termites, where male becomes "king" alongside his "queen"); queen ant stores all sperm needed for fertilizing many eggs over a long period

Diet Adults feed mainly on nectar and honeydew or on fungus; larvae eat food of animal (mainly insect) or plant (mainly seed) origin; sole diet for some species is a fungus that they cultivate in special "gardens"

Habitat Found in all terrestrial habitats, where they are often dominant; no aquatic species

Distribution Worldwide; commonest in the tropics, absent from very dry or cold areas

Spider Wasps

The European spider-hunting wasp, *Anoplius nigerinus*, preys on wolf spiders (Arachnida: Lycosidae). Having paralyzed the spider with her formidable sting, the female wasp drags it to the nest site to be used as food for her larvae. Body length 0.4 inches (10 mm).

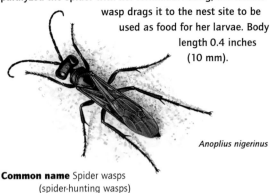

Anoplius nigerinus

Common name Spider wasps (spider-hunting wasps)

Family Pompilidae

Suborder Apocrita

Order Hymenoptera

Class/Subphylum Insecta/Hexapoda

Number of species About 4,000 (about 250–300 U.S.)

Size From about 0.4 in (10 mm) to about 2 in (5 cm)

Key features Body slim or fairly stout; glossy, often blue-black, frequently marked with red or yellow; both sexes fully winged; wings often cloudy; long legs built for running fast; eyes entire; antennae with 12 segments in females, 13 in males; pronotum extends backward to base of wings; wings flat when held at rest over back

Habits Active in daytime, preferring high temperatures; females usually seen looking for spiders or dragging them over the ground; males mostly found on flowers

Breeding Males much smaller than females; females of some species lay eggs on spiders, then retire; larva eats still-active spider; in most species females stock larval nest cavity with a single large spider that has been paralyzed by stinging

Diet Adults feed on nectar from flowers; larvae eat spiders

Habitat Most common in dry, open habitats such as deserts, dunes, and grassy hillsides; also in rain forests and other wooded habitats

Distribution Worldwide, but commonest in warmer regions

Social Wasps

The yellow jacket, *Vespula germanica* (also known as the German wasp), builds its nest in suitable buildings or underground and is common in Europe. Body length (of worker) 0.9 inches (22 mm).

Yellow jacket
(Vespula germanica)

Common name
Social wasps
(paper wasps, potter wasps)

Family Vespidae

Suborder Apocrita

Order Hymenoptera

Class/Subphylum Insecta/Hexapoda

Number of species About 4,000 (about 415 U.S.)

Size From about 0.2 in (5 mm) to about 1.4 in (3.5 cm)

Key features Body usually banded, often black and yellow or black and white; sometimes all black or brown, occasionally green; eyes with a distinct notch at the front; both sexes fully winged; pronotum reaches back to the wing bases; wings pleated when held at rest over back; females armed with stinger

Habits Mostly active during the day, a few species nocturnal; adults hunt for larval food on leaves or flowers; paper wasp nests often conspicuous on buildings; potter wasps may be conspicuous collecting mud around puddles

Breeding Potter wasps are solitary and build mud nests, which they fill with spiders; paper wasps are highly social; nests often large, usually made of "paper," in which overlapping generations of workers care for the young and eventually rear males and future queens; nests may be founded and dominated by one or more queens

Diet Adults mainly eat nectar from flowers, honeydew, juices oozing from ripe fruits, and leaking sap on tree trunks; larvae are mainly carnivorous

Habitat Common in all kinds of terrestrial habitats that are not too dry or cold

Distribution Worldwide, commonest in the tropics

Solitary Wasps

Mellinus arvensis from Europe, known as the fly-hunting wasp or the field digger wasp, is seen here paralyzing a fly roughly the same size as itself, which will shortly provide a meal for the larvae. Body length 0.5 inches (13 mm).

Fly-hunting wasp
(Mellinus arvensis)

Common name Solitary wasps (hunting wasps)

Family Sphecidae

Suborder Apocrita

Order Hymenoptera

Class/Subphylum Insecta/Hexapoda

Number of species Over 7,700 (about 1,200 U.S.)

Size From about 0.1 in (2.5 mm) to about 2.2 in (5.5 cm)

Key features Color varied: usually striped black and yellow or black and white, often plain brown or black, sometimes with broad reddish band; body shape variable, mostly typically wasplike but also long and thin; pronotum does not extend backward to base of wings (unlike in Pompilidae and Vespidae); sting present in females; wings not pleated when held at rest

Habits Active in daytime; adults of both sexes—but especially males—may be found on flowers; females mostly seen digging nests or dragging prey back to the nest; some species build communal mud nests

Breeding Mating takes place at nest sites, on flowers, or at landmarks such as hilltops; females build nests in the ground or in cavities such as hollow twigs, old beetle borings, and other concealed places; nests stocked with paralyzed invertebrates, mostly insects

Diet Adults mainly feed on nectar or honeydew; females may also sup on fluids oozing from their prey or on its crop contents; larvae feed on insects and spiders; most species only take specific kinds of prey

Habitat Most common in dry, warm, open habitats such as deserts; also often abundant on bare city lots, sports fields, in backyards, on roadsides, in woodlands, and most kinds of habitats; less conspicuous in dense forest

Distribution Worldwide; most common in warm, dry regions

Leaf-Cutter Bees and Relatives

The European wool-carder bee, *Anthidium manicatum*, builds its nest in cavities in wood or masonry, lining it with a cottonlike fluff "carded" from the leaves and stems of hairy plants. Body length of female 0.4 inches (10 mm); male 0.6 inches (15 mm).

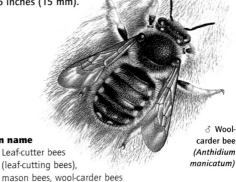

♂ Wool-carder bee (*Anthidium manicatum*)

Common name
 Leaf-cutter bees (leaf-cutting bees), mason bees, wool-carder bees

Family Megachilidae

Suborder Apocrita

Order Hymenoptera

Class/Subphylum Insecta/Hexapoda

Number of species Over 3,500 (about 600 U.S.)

Size From 0.4 in (10 mm) to 1.6 in (4 cm)

Key features Body stoutly built, usually hairy; gray or brown, sometimes boldly marked in black and yellow or black and orange; pollen carried on brush of hairs (scopa) on the underside of the abdomen, rather than on the hind legs as in most other bees; tongue long and slender

Habits Usually seen collecting pollen from flowers, cutting leaves or gathering other materials to line nests, or digging nests in ground; some species are cuckoos in nests of others

Breeding Males of some species are territorial around flowers or nests; females build nests in tunnels in the ground or in natural cavities in wood or stone; leaf-cutter females cut sections of leaf with which to build cells; mason bees build cells with mud; wool-carder bees collect fluffy plant material or animal hairs as nest-lining materials

Diet Adults feed on nectar from a variety of flowers; larvae feed on pollen and nectar collected by adults

Habitat Most common in open habitats, rarer in dense forest, but present in all terrestrial habitats; several species often common in gardens and may nest inside greenhouses

Distribution Worldwide except in very cold or dry zones

Mining Bees

A solitary mining bee, *Colletes succinctus*, and her cluster of cells, each with an egg attached to the cell wall. When they hatch, the larvae drop into the liquid mixture of honey and pollen below. Length 0.4 inches (10 mm).

Colletes succinctus

Common name Mining bees

Family Andrenidae

Suborder Apocrita

Order Hymenoptera

Class/Subphylum Insecta/Hexapoda

Number of species About 5,000
(about 1,200 U.S.)

Size From about 0.4 in
(10 mm) to about
0.6 in (15 mm)

Key features Mainly hairy
bees, mostly dark
brown or rusty
brown, some black;
mainly hairless in
subfamily Panurginae; tongue
short but pointed at the tip

Habits Both sexes normally found on flowers; they carry nectar
and pollen back to the nest on the hind legs; some
species are cuckoos in the nests of others

Breeding Females build nests by digging vertical tunnels in the
ground, occasionally in dense aggregations with other
females; a few species are communal, with several
females using parts of a single nest system; males often
a different color from females

Diet Adults feed on nectar from many different kinds of
flowers; larvae supplied with nectar and pollen, often
from only a single species of flower or several closely
related species in a single family

Habitat All terrestrial habitats and often among the commonest
bees in gardens, especially in springtime; prefer open
habitats; common in deserts, rare in dense forest

Distribution Widespread on all continents except Australia
and Antarctica

Digger Bees and Carpenter Bees

The female of the carpenter bee, *Xylocopa violacea*, makes her nest in dead trees. The species is found in central and southern Europe, and is nonaggressive.
Body length 0.7 inches
(19 mm).

Carpenter bee
(*Xylocopa violacea*)

Common name Digger bees, carpenter bees

Family Anthophoridae

Suborder Apocrita

Order Hymenoptera

Class/Subphylum Insecta/Hexapoda

Number of species Over 4,000 (about 920 U.S.)

Size From about 0.2 in (6 mm) to about 1 in (2.5 cm)

Key features Body extremely varied: often large, robust, and densely hairy, similar to bumblebees; some species bright sky blue, others small, slim, and resembling wasps, with black-and-yellow bands; wings have distinctive veins; tongue in some species very long, sometimes longer than body

Habits Habits as varied as appearance; larger species visit flowers to gather pollen, nectar, or oils; many species are cuckoos in the nests of others; most are solitary, a few are communal, some are relatively social

Breeding Males find females in a number of ways; males of some genera are noted for their long antennae; females mainly construct nests in the ground, lining burrows with secretions from Dufour's gland on abdomen; some species nest in wood, others only in sides of termite mounds in tropics

Diet Adults feed on nectar; larvae feed on mixture of pollen and nectar or pollen mixed with plant oils

Habitat All kinds of habitat, from rain forest to mountain top and desert to town garden; some species nest in walls or the structural timbers of buildings

Distribution Worldwide in habitable areas

Honeybees and Relatives

The honeybee *Apis mellifera* is found worldwide thanks to commercial beekeeping. It plays an important role in plant reproduction, transferring pollen from plant to plant. Body length (of worker) 0.5 inches (13 mm).

Apis mellifera

Common name
Honeybees, stingless bees, bumblebees, orchid bees

Family Apidae

Suborder Apocrita

Order Hymenoptera

Class/Subphylum Insecta/Hexapoda

Number of species About 1,000 (60 U.S.)

Size From about 0.08 in (2 mm) to about 1.1 in (2.7 cm)

Key features Small, hairless, mainly brown or black body (stingless bees); medium-sized, slim-waisted, brown body (honeybees); stout and densely hairy rusty brown or black body, often with red or yellow bands (bumblebees); brilliant metallic-blue or green body, sometimes hairy like bumblebees (orchid bees); tongue long; pollen baskets generally present on hind legs

Habits Most species common on flowers and are important pollinators of many crops; honeybee often domesticated in hives

Breeding Most species often highly social, living in large nests containing thousands of workers (nonbreeding females); social species eventually rear males and females who leave nest for mating purposes; mated queens then found new nest, usually in following spring after winter hibernation; some species are cuckoos in nests of others

Diet Adults feed mainly on nectar; in tropics orchid bees and stingless bees often feed on dung or urine-soaked ground; larvae eat pollen and nectar; larvae of some stingless bees eat carrion

Habitat In all terrestrial habitats from sea level to vegetation limits on mountains; many species common in gardens

Distribution Worldwide in areas that are not too arid or permanently cold; honeybee introduced into the Americas, Australia, and New Zealand

Springtails

Springtails such as *Orchesella cincta* from the Northern Hemisphere often occur in concealed, damp places and on the surface of ponds. They feed on decomposing organic matter, and some use their biting mouthparts to feed on living plants. Size: 0.1 in (2.5 mm).

Orchesella cincta

Common name
  Springtails

Class Collembola

Subphylum Hexapoda

Number of species More than 8,000 (677 U.S.)

Size From less than 0.04 in (1 mm) to 0.5 in (12 mm)

Key features Body soft, rounded to elongate in shape; may be pure white, variably colored, or metallic; mouthparts long and positioned inside head, can be pushed out to feed; eyes poorly developed; 3 pairs of walking legs; wings absent; abdomen has only 6 segments and in most species carries a jumping structure, the furcula

Habits Prefer to stay out of sight in dark, damp places where food is present, e.g., under stones, in rotting wood, in compost heaps, in leaf litter, in the soil, in caves, and in ant and termite nests; some species are day-active on plants

Breeding Males deposit spermatophores for females to pick up; courtship known in some species

Diet Decaying vegetable matter, including fungi

Habitat Found in all kinds of habitat as long as it is moist; some species live on the surface of water, even the sea

Distribution Worldwide, even on the surface of snowfields

Silverfish

Thermobia domestica is a common species of silverfish with worldwide distribution. It is particularly fond of warm habitats and can be found, for example, inside buildings close to ovens and heating systems. Length from head to tail tip 0.8 inches (2 cm).

Thermobia domestica

Common name
Silverfish, fire brats

Order Thysanura

Class Insecta

Subphylum Hexapoda

Number of species About 370 (18 U.S.)

Size From about 0.3 in (7 mm) to 0.5 in (13 mm)

Key features Fairly obvious head, thorax, and abdomen; body shape generally long, slim, and tapering from head to tail, slightly flattened, often covered in scales; head bears long antennae; eyes simple; biting jaws present; 3 pairs of legs on thorax; wings lacking; 3 long "tails" present on the end of the abdomen

Habits Tend to live in dark places where it is reasonably damp, but not wet; generally nocturnal

Breeding Some simple courtship known; males deposit spermatophores for females to pick up

Diet Decaying vegetable matter of all kinds; is able to digest cellulose

Habitat Forests, caves, and human habitations

Distribution Worldwide

Mayflies

The subimago, or preadult stage, of *Leptophlebia marginata* is known to fly fishermen as the sepia dun. Found across northern and central Europe, it is used as bait to catch trout. Length 0.4 inches (1 cm).

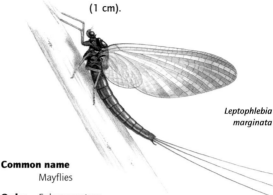

Leptophlebia marginata

Common name
  Mayflies

Order Ephemeroptera

Class Insecta

Subphylum Hexapoda

Number of species More than 2,000 (611 U.S.)

Size From about 0.2 in (5 mm) to 1.2 in (3 cm)

Key features Adults with 2 pairs of membranous wings, the first pair much larger than the second, which may be absent altogether in some species; at the end of the abdomen are 3 long "tails" (2 in some families); large compound eyes; antennae short; mouthparts reduced; nymphs have well-developed jaws and also 3 "tails"

Habits Adults spend their short lives on vegetation near water or in courtship swarms; nymphs are usually nocturnal and aquatic, living in all types of fresh water, but not if it is too stagnant; nymphs undergo unique, preadult winged stage (the subimago)

Breeding Usually form mating swarms; males grab females in midair; both males and females usually present, but a few species use parthenogenesis; eggs laid in water

Diet Nymphs mainly vegetarian; adults do not feed

Habitat Ponds, lakes, streams, rivers, and canals; a few species live in brackish water

Distribution Worldwide, especially in temperate zones

Dragonflies and Damselflies

A female southern hawker, *Aeshna cyanea*, lays her eggs in a soft, water-logged tree stump. (*Aeshna* means ugly or misshapen and *cyanea* means dark blue, although there is no blue color present in the female of the species.) The southern hawker is widespread throughout Europe. Wingspan up to 3.5 inches (9 cm) and body length up to 2.8 inches (7 cm).

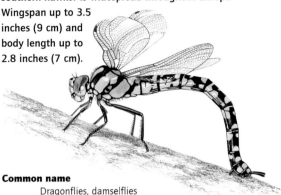

♀ Southern hawker (*Aeshna cyanea*)

Common name
  Dragonflies, damselflies

Order Odonata

Class Insecta

Subphylum Hexapoda

Number of species About 6,500 (438 U.S.)

Size From about 0.7 in (19 mm) to 5 in (13 cm)

Key features Head with large compound eyes and well-developed jaws; antennae very short; 2 pairs of transparent wings almost equal in size; abdomen long and slim in most species; dragonflies hold their wings out to the side, damselflies fold their wings over and along the body; jaws in nymphs can be extended for grabbing prey; damselfly nymphs have 3 external gills, dragonfly nymphs have gills inside the rectum

Habits Damselflies normally found hunting for prey close to water; stronger-flying dragonflies may often be found hunting a long way from water; nymphs mostly aquatic

Breeding Males may grab females in midair or pounce on sitting females; some species have complex courtship routines; eggs laid in or near water

Diet Both adults and nymphs are predators

Habitat Any habitat with suitable still or running water, the latter not too fast; some species can inhabit deserts provided water is available at least for a short time

Distribution Found all over the world except for the North and South Poles

Walkingsticks and Leaf Insects

Acrophylla titan, aptly named the titan stick insect or the great brown phasma, is the longest Australian species. The females are generally much larger than the males and are abundant egg layers. Two captive females were observed to lay over 4,000 eggs between them during their lifetime. Body length up to 10 inches (25 cm).

Titan stick insect
(Acrophylla titan)

Common name
Walkingsticks (stick insects), leaf insects, timemas

Order Phasmatodea (Phasmida)

Class Insecta

Subphylum Hexapoda

Number of species About 2,500 (32 U.S.)

Size From about 0.5 in (13 mm) to 13 in (33 cm)

Key features Body shape anything from short and broad in leaf insects to very long and thin in walkingsticks; antennae slim, very variable in length; compound eyes fairly small; simple eyes in flying species but often only present in the male; wings (when present) usually only full size in males, many species wingless in both sexes; forewings leathery to protect hind wings; nymphs resemble adults, but are wingless

Habits Almost all species sit around on vegetation and are active at night

Breeding Courtship mainly absent; many males guard the female during egg laying; eggs dropped anywhere or inserted into crevices

Diet All species feed on living vegetation of some kind

Habitat Forests, grassy areas, scrub, semidesert, and desert

Distribution Worldwide, but most common in the tropics; absent from cool, temperate regions

Earwigs

The tawny earwig, *Labidura riparia*, sometimes flies to lights at night and can emit an unpleasant smell when captured. It is found across the southern United States. Length up to 1 inch (2.5 cm).

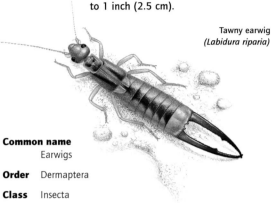

Tawny earwig
(Labidura riparia)

Common name
Earwigs

Order Dermaptera

Class Insecta

Subphylum Hexapoda

Number of species About 1,800 (20 U.S.)

Size From about 0.2 in (5 mm) to 1 in (2.5 cm)

Key features Relatively elongate, rather flattened body; head with large or small compound eyes (or lacking eyes) and biting and chewing jaws; winged or wingless; forewings only very small; hind wings semicircular in shape, folding up neatly to fit beneath the forewing covers; cerci highly modified to form "pincers"; nymphs resemble adults

Habits Most are nocturnal; some live in burrows, a few unusual species live on mammals

Breeding Males of some species use the pincers to hold the female; parental care by females not uncommon

Diet Feed as scavengers on a variety of dead and decaying organic matter; some eat flowers; a few are semiparasitic

Habitat Grassland, forests, deserts, and gardens

Distribution Worldwide

Termites

A soldier-caste *Nasutitermes* sp. termite, known as a "nasute" soldier. The species is found in forest undergrowth in lowland areas of Central and South America. Length 0.2 inches (5 mm).

Nasutitermes sp.

Common name
Termites
(white ants)

Order Isoptera

Class Insecta

Subphylum Hexapoda

Number of species About 2,300 (44 U.S.)

Size From about 0.2 in (5 mm) to 1 in (2.5 cm)

Key features Social insects with kings, queens, soldiers, and workers; jaws typically used for biting and chewing; compound eyes (may be reduced or absent); antennae slim and about the same length as the thorax; membranous wings present in sexual forms, absent in workers and soldiers; soldiers often with large jaws or a snoutlike extension of the head; nymphs resemble wingless adults

Habits Social insects with colonies of up to millions of individuals; live in the ground, often within mounds, or burrow into wood

Breeding Winged sexual forms fly from colonies; females land and release pheromones to attract males; queens lay large numbers of eggs and are fed and looked after by workers

Diet Fungi and decaying plant material

Habitat Forests, savanna, semidesert, and desert

Distribution Worldwide, but mainly tropical; just a few species in warm, temperate zones

Cockroaches

The American cockroach, *Periplaneta americana*, is also known as the waterbug because of its preference for living in damp places such as water pipes and sewage systems. It is thought to have been introduced to the United States from Africa as early as 1625 and has spread across the world by crawling into grocery packages and being transported to new locations. Body length 1.5–2 inches (3.8–5 cm).

American cockroach
(*Periplaneta americana*)

Common name
Cockroaches

Order Blattodea

Class Insecta

Subphylum Hexapoda

Number of species Around 4,000 (over 50 U.S.)

Size From about 0.15 in (4 mm) to 4.8 in (12 cm)

Key features Body tends to be rather flattened; head with well-developed compound eyes (except cave dwellers), long, thin antennae with many segments, and chewing mouthparts; pronotum usually forms a shield over the thorax and may extend forward to cover the top of the head; forewings toughened, covering the membranous hind wings; wings may be absent, especially in females; 1 pair of cerci on the end of the abdomen; nymphs resemble wingless adults

Habits Many species are nocturnal, while some come out in the day and feed from flowers

Breeding Mating may be preceded by courtship; stridulation (hissing) is known to occur in some species; eggs laid in a special purselike structure, the ootheca; parental care is known for a number of species

Diet Scavengers; many species will eat almost anything edible that they come across

Habitat Grassland, forests, deserts, sand dunes, caves, and human habitations

Distribution Worldwide, but most species found in the tropics

Mantids

The praying mantis, *Mantis religiosa*, is found waiting for smaller insect prey on flowers and foliage. It was accidentally introduced from southern Europe into the United States in 1899. Length including wings 2.5 inches (6 cm).

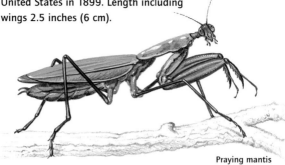

Praying mantis
(*Mantis religiosa*)

Common name Mantids
(praying mantises)

Order Mantodea

Class Insecta

Subphylum Hexapoda

Number of species About 2,000 (20 U.S.)

Size From about 0.4 in (10 mm) to 6 in (15 cm)

Key features Males normally smaller than females; head roughly triangular when seen from front; eyes large and well separated; antennae thin; jaws for cutting and chewing prey; head held well away from the body on elongated first thoracic segment; front legs adapted for grasping prey; forewings leathery, covering membranous hind wings; 1 pair of cerci on the end of the abdomen; nymphs resemble adults or are ant mimics, at least in the early instars

Habits Most species sit on vegetation waiting for prey; some sit on bark, others live on the ground

Breeding Females attract males to them—courtship follows; eggs laid in a special purselike structure, the ootheca; maternal care known in some species

Diet Predators, feeding on other insects and also spiders; occasionally take small vertebrates such as lizards

Habitat Grassland, scrub, forests, semideserts, and deserts

Distribution Mainly tropical in distribution, with a few species in warmer temperate areas

Stoneflies

The European stonefly, *Perla bipunctata*, is an impressive insect with distinctive yellow markings. It takes three years to mature and up to 30 molts to reach full size. It can be found on rivers and streams, but rarely on ponds. Body length up to 1.6 inches (4 cm).

European stonefly
(Perla bipunctata)

Common name Stoneflies

Order Plecoptera

Class Insecta

Subphylum Hexapoda

Number of species About 2,000 (465 U.S.)

Size From about 0.2 in (5 mm) to 2.5 in (6 cm)

Key features Adults fairly slim bodied, with a cylindrical appearance; head has 2 long, thin antennae and large, bulging compound eyes; chewing mouthparts present but never used; wings membranous, hind wings larger than forewings, wrapped around body and often much longer than the abdomen; some species lack wings, or they may be reduced in size in males; 1 pair of slim cerci, often quite long, on the end of the abdomen; nymphs look like wingless adults but with jaws for feeding; nymphs have gills on the abdomen

Habits Adults always found near water and are often nocturnal; nymphs usually found in well-oxygenated water

Breeding Males and females drum to one another during courtship; eggs laid into water

Diet Some adults do not feed, others eat algae and lichens; nymphs feed either on vegetable matter or more often on other small water creatures

Habitat Fast-flowing rivers and streams and wave-lapped lakesides; just a few species in stiller waters

Distribution Most species found in the cooler, temperate areas of the world

Web Spinners

The web spinner *Haploembia solieri* (family Oligotomidae) comes from the Mediterranean region. The males have two pairs of long narrow wings, but the females are always wingless. Size 0.4–0.5 in (10–13 mm).

Haploembia solieri

Common name Web spinners

Order Embioptera

Class Insecta

Subphylum Hexapoda

Number of species About 200 (9 U.S.)

Size From about 0.1 in (3 mm) to 0.5 in (13 mm)

Key features Long, slim body; females wingless, males with or without wings; head bears threadlike antennae; small compound eyes (tiny in females) and chewing jaws; winged males have 2 pairs of similar-sized, smoky wings; powerful hind legs for running backward; front tarsi enlarged to produce silk

Habits Live in silken tunnels under stones, bark, or leaf litter, which they seldom leave; may form colonies with interconnecting tunnels

Breeding Males hold females in their jaws during mating; females show parental care of eggs and young nymphs

Diet Moss and decaying vegetable matter

Habitat Forests, screes, and piles of stones

Distribution Mainly tropical and subtropical zones

Thrips

The western flower thrips, *Frankliniella occidentalis*, is a destructive pest of numerous greenhouse and nursery crops. It damages the leaves and flowers of the plants, and can carry diseases, such as the tomato spotted virus, which attacks many vegetables. The species is known worldwide. Body length 0.04 inches (1–2 mm).

Western flower thrips (*Frankliniella occidentalis*)

Common name Thrips
(thunder bugs)

Order Thysanoptera

Class Insecta

Subphylum Hexapoda

Number of species About 5,000 (700 U.S.)

Size From about 0.02 in (0.5 mm) to 0.6 in (15 mm)

Key features Body long and slim; head with compound eyes and sucking mouthparts; antennae short; both fore- and hind wings, when present, are barlike with fringes of hairs; hind legs used for jumping; nymphs resemble adults, but are wingless

Habits Many live on flowers and developing seed heads; some form galls in plant tissues; others live on fungi; may disperse in their millions on warm days

Breeding Reproduce both sexually and by laying unfertilized eggs; males of many species fight each other for females

Diet The majority are plant and fungus feeders, while a few are predaceous

Habitat Forests, grassland, gardens, cultivated fields, orchards, deserts, and semideserts

Distribution Worldwide

Booklice and Barklice

Liposcelis terricolis thrives in damp conditions. This booklouse is found worldwide. The swollen femora on the hind legs are distinctive features of the species. Body length 0.2 inches (5 mm).

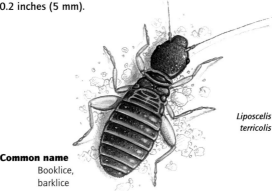

Liposcelis terricolis

Common name
> Booklice, barklice

Order Psocoptera

Class Insecta

Subphylum Hexapoda

Number of species About 3,200 (245 U.S.)

Size From around 0.08 in (2 mm) to 0.4 in (10 mm)

Key features Head with a pair of thin antennae and compound eyes; simple eyes present in barklice, but not in booklice; mouthparts adapted for chewing; legs quite long for fast running; booklice lack wings, barklice have 2 pairs of membranous wings, sometimes colored; hind wings larger than front pair; cerci lacking

Habits Wingless species favor dark places under stones and bark, in leaf litter, or within crevices in houses and sheds; winged species live on bark and among vegetation

Breeding Males of some species stridulate; courtship dances are known to occur; eggs laid in clusters

Diet All kinds of vegetable matter, fungi, stored food products, and book bindings

Habitat Forests, desert and semidesert, birds' nests, human dwellings, and storehouses

Distribution Worldwide

Lice

Trichodectes canis, the dog louse, is found all over the world. Large infestations of the parasite can cause considerable irritation to dogs (especially pups), which will try in vain to remove the pests by scratching vigorously. Body length 0.04 inches (1 mm).

Dog louse
(Trichodectes canis)

Common name Lice

Order Phthiraptera

Class Insecta

Subphylum Hexapoda

Number of species About 5,500 (1,000 U.S.)

Size From about 0.02 in (0.5 mm) to 0.4 in (10 mm)

Key features Flattened, wingless insects; antennae short; eyes small or absent; mouthparts used for chewing in 2 suborders and for sucking in the 3rd suborder; legs with strong claws on the foot to grasp the hair or feathers of host mammals and birds; nymphs are like tiny pale adults

Habits Live on or near their host birds or mammals, which include humans

Breeding Eggs are attached to the hair or feathers of host animals

Diet Feed either on bird feathers or mammal skin, or suck blood

Habitat Found wherever their hosts are, as well as terrestrial mammals and birds; hosts also include seals, penguins, and oceanic birds that only come to land to breed

Distribution Worldwide

Lacewings and Relatives

Libelloides coccajus is a distinctive lacewing. It looks like a small dragonfly, with long antennae and yellow-and-black wings. The species, found mainly in Europe, is highly predatory on other insects. Body length 0.75 inches (18 mm).

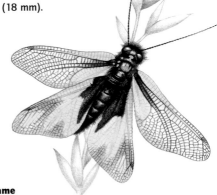

Libelloides coccajus

Common name
Lacewings, mantid flies, ant lions, owlflies, butterfly lions

Order Neuroptera

Class Insecta

Subphylum Hexapoda

Number of species About 4,500 (285 U.S.)

Size From about 0.2 in (5 mm) to 1.8 in (4.6 cm)

Key features Adult head has longish, slim antennae, sometimes with knobs at the end; compound eyes vary from small to very large in relation to size of head; chewing jaws present; both pairs of wings membranous and held tentlike over abdomen; larvae usually with large mandibles, sometimes covered in detritus; pupa usually encased in a silk cocoon

Habits Many are nocturnal; virtually all have a weak, rather flappy flight; some day fliers may be mistaken for butterflies; larvae found on all sorts of vegetation, including bark, and on or in the ground

Breeding Courtship can be quite complex; eggs, which may be on long stalks of hardened mucus, laid on vegetation

Diet Adults predaceous, but some also take pollen and nectar; larvae predaceous

Habitat Forests, orchards, savanna, grassland, sand dunes, semidesert, and desert

Distribution Worldwide

Alderflies and Dobsonflies

Sialis lutaria is a European alderfly that appears in early summer. The adults prefer to live on trees or plants close to water, especially the alder—hence the name alderfly. Body length up to 1 inch (2.5 cm).

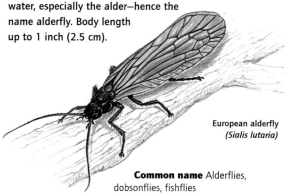

European alderfly
(Sialis lutaria)

Common name Alderflies, dobsonflies, fishflies

Order Megaloptera

Class Insecta

Subphylum Hexapoda

Number of species About 300 (45 U.S.)

Size From about 0.4 in (10 mm) to 2.8 in (7 cm)

Key features Antennae threadlike, can be serrated or comblike in some fishflies; jaws small in alderflies, larger in female dobsonflies, and very large in male dobsonflies; compound eyes present; wings membranous, smoky in alderflies and some fishflies, and held tentlike over the abdomen in all cases; larvae with chewing jaws and thin filaments sticking out from the side of abdominal segments

Habits Adults usually found on vegetation near water; larvae aquatic; alderflies usually active by day; dobsonflies and fishflies nocturnal

Breeding Both sound and visual cues known to be involved in courtship; eggs laid on rocks or vegetation near water

Diet Adults not known to feed; larvae are predaceous on aquatic insects and their larvae, also on worms

Habitat Ponds, lakes, rivers, and streams; also swamps, water in rot holes in trees, and in pitcher plants

Distribution Worldwide in unpolluted waters

Snakeflies

The Texas snakefly, *Agulla nixa*, is found in Texas and adjacent areas of Mexico, where it inhabits woods. It feeds on smaller insects, and the female lays eggs into bark crevices with her long ovipositor. Body length 0.6–0.9 inches (15–22 mm).

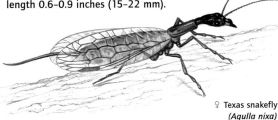

♀ Texas snakefly
(Agulla nixa)

Common name Snakeflies

Order Raphidioptera

Class Insecta

Subphylum Hexapoda

Number of species About 206 (19 U.S.)

Size From about in 0.5 in (13 mm) to 0.7 in (18 mm)

Key features Head long and flattened with compound eyes, long, slim antennae, and chewing jaws at the front; first thoracic segment is long, keeping the head away from the rest of the body and giving the appearance of a snake's head; 2 pairs of similar-sized membranous wings held tentlike along the body; female with long ovipositor on abdomen

Habits Adults most often found on trees; larvae live in leaf litter and beneath bark

Breeding Mating behavior differs between the 2 main families; female uses long ovipositor to lay eggs in soil litter or beneath tree bark

Diet Both adults and larvae feed on small, soft-bodied insects such as aphids; some adults also eat pollen

Habitat Forests and other dense stands of trees

Distribution Across the Northern Hemisphere; where they occur in the tropics, they are usually at higher levels or on mountains

Centipedes

Scutigera coleoptrata, the house centipede, is a species from Europe, but now has been introduced and is widespread in the United States and Mexico. It lives indoors and outdoors, but is the only centipede that can reproduce indoors. It preys on other insects and, with its 15 pairs of legs, is an extremely fast runner. Body length up to 1.5 inches (3.8 cm).

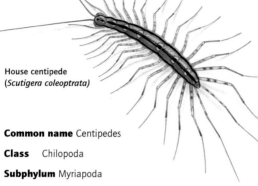

House centipede
(*Scutigera coleoptrata*)

Common name Centipedes

Class   Chilopoda

Subphylum Myriapoda

Number of species About 2,500 (not known U.S)

Size   From about 0.4 in (10 mm) to 10 in (25 cm)

Key features Body formed from head and multisegmented trunk; each trunk segment (except the first and last 2) has a pair of legs; appendages on first trunk segment modified to inject poison into prey; head has a pair of slim antennae and chewing mouthparts (1 pair of mandibles and 2 pairs of maxillae); eyes, when present, simple or compound

Habits   Mainly nocturnal, when they can be found moving around the habitat they live in looking for prey; 1 family lives in the soil, moving around in worm burrows and natural cracks

Breeding Courtship described for some species; otherwise males leave spermatophores lying around for females to collect; female parental care is known in some species

Diet   Mainly carnivorous, but some soil dwellers feed on vegetable matter

Habitat Grassland, forests, semideserts, and deserts

Distribution Worldwide

Millipedes

A giant millipede, order Spirostreptida, curled up in a defensive coil. The Spirostreptida are subtropical and tropical millipedes. Length 0.5 inches (13 cm) to 11 inches (28 cm).

Giant millipede
(order Spirostreptida)

Common name Millipedes

Class Diplopoda

Subphylum Myriapoda

Number of species About 10,000 (2,167 U.S.)

Size From about 0.16 in (4 mm) to 12 in (30 cm)

Key features Head with 1 pair of very short antennae, 1 pair of eyes, and chewing mouthparts; body shape very variable, from long and cylindrical to short and humped or long and flattened; all have many segments with 2 pairs of legs per segment; some species can roll up into a ball when threatened

Breeding Courtship rituals are quite common; some males use sound communication to attract the female; female usually makes some form of nest in which eggs are laid and then left

Diet Plant material, especially if it is dead and decaying

Habitat Forests, grassland, desert and semidesert, mountains, and gardens

Distribution Worldwide, but commoner in tropical regions

Caddisflies

An adult of the great red sedge, *Phryganea grandis*, a European species found as far north as Lapland. The larvae build their protective cases with plant material arranged in a spiral. Body length 0.5 inches (13 mm).

Great red sedge
(Phryganea grandis)

Common name Caddisflies

Order Trichoptera

Class Insecta

Subphylum Hexapoda

Number of species About 7,000 (1,262 U.S.)

Size From about 0.06 in (1.5 mm) to 1 in (2.5 cm)

Key features Adults mothlike, with a slender, elongate body; most species drably colored in all shades of brown to black, a few brightly colored; body and wings hairy; wings held tentlike over the body; head bears threadlike antennae that can be 2 or 3 times the body length; large compound eyes used in locating each other; mouthparts reduced or almost nonexistent; most larvae similar to caterpillars, living in cases or silken tubes; some free-living, without a case

Habits Adults often nocturnal, usually found on vegetation near water; most larvae aquatic, living in water of all kinds

Breeding Males often form huge mating swarms over or near water; eggs laid in, near, or under water

Diet Adults either do not feed or just take liquid food; larvae may be vegetarian or predaceous

Habitat Lakes, ponds, streams, and rivers

Distribution Worldwide

Scorpionflies and Hangingflies

The large scorpionfly *Panorpa nuptialis* occurs mainly in the south-central United States and Mexico. This popular species made recent appearances on postage stamps in the United States and the United Arab Emirates. Length up to 0.8 inches (20 mm).

Panorpa nuptialis

Common name
Scorpionflies, hangingflies

Order Mecoptera

Class Insecta

Subphylum Hexapoda

Number of species About 500 (about 80 U.S.)

Size From about 0.08 in (2 mm) to 1 in (2.5 cm)

Key features Long, beaklike face at the end of which are the chewing mouthparts; antennae long and slim; compound eyes large; both pairs of wings similar in size, membranous, often with dark markings; some species wingless; male reproductive structures often enlarged, resembling a scorpion sting in scorpionflies

Habits Scorpionflies are scavengers searching for dead insects on which to feed; hangingflies hang on vegetation waiting to snatch passing insects

Breeding Courtship can be complex in all families; male hangingflies provide gifts to their mates; females lay eggs into soil or moss

Diet Scorpionfly adults and larvae eat dead insects, but some are vegetarian; hangingfly adults and larvae are predaceous; snow scorpionflies are vegetarians

Habitat Forests, hedgerows, parks, gardens, and mountains

Distribution Worldwide

Fleas

The dog flea, *Ctenocephalides canis*, and the cat flea, *Ctenocephalides felis*, are probably the most common domestic fleas, with a worldwide distribution. The flea life cycle takes about three weeks, but eggs can remain dormant for long periods in cool weather. Length w0.1 inches (3–4 mm).

Dog flea
(Ctenocephalides canis)

Common name
Fleas

Order Siphonaptera

Class Insecta

Subphylum Hexapoda

Number of species About 2,380 (325 U.S.)

Size From about 0.04 in (1 mm) to 0.5 in (13 mm)

Key features Adults very flattened from side to side; wingless; hind legs modified for jumping; head without compound eyes; simple eyes may be absent or well developed; mouthparts adapted for sucking blood

Habits Adults live on their hosts; hosts are mainly mammals, but also a few birds; larvae live in nests or close to where the hosts live

Breeding Breeding cycle of fleas often linked to that of the host; eggs normally laid in the host's nest or living area

Diet Blood for the adults, shed skin and other edible bits and pieces for the larvae

Habitat Wherever the hosts are found

Distribution Worldwide

Water Fleas and Fairy Shrimps

The powerful second antennae of the *Daphnia* water flea make jerking downstrokes that propel the tiny animal up through the water. Five eggs can be seen clearly in the brood pouch of this female. Length up to 0.1 inches (3 mm).

♀ *Daphnia* sp.

Common name Water fleas, fairy shrimps (also brine, clam, and tadpole shrimps)

Class Branchiopoda

Subphylum Crustacea

Number of species About 800 species representing 23 families in 3 orders

Size 0.01 in (0.3 mm) to 4 in (10 cm)

Key features A diverse group characterized by paddlelike appendages on segmented trunk, with gills growing from leg bases; first antennae and second maxillae are vestigial; abdomen has paired "tails" called cercopods; carapace may or may not be present

Habits Swim using antennae or trunk appendages, or crawl on surface; often phototactic (attracted to light); populations often cyclical, with peaks in warm, wet seasons

Breeding Most species reproduce parthenogenetically, with males only appearing when population is under stress; females produce 2 kinds of eggs—summer eggs develop immediately, winter (resistant) eggs may lie dormant for many years

Diet Mostly suspension feeders on bacteria, algae, and detritus; occasionally feed on multicellular plant material and carrion; some water fleas are predatory

Habitat Mostly in temporary fresh water such as puddles, dew ponds, and seasonal lakes; water fleas live in permanent streams and lakes; some water fleas and brine shrimps are adapted to brackish and salty water

Distribution Worldwide

Barnacles

The acorn barnacle, *Semibalanus balanoides*—a European species—grows on rocks on the middle and lower shore. Its shape varies according to habitat, growing more columnar in crowded populations. Diameter about 0.4 inches (10 mm).

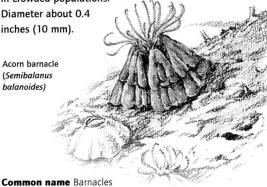

Acorn barnacle
(*Semibalanus balanoides*)

Common name Barnacles

Infraclass Cirripedia

Class Maxillopoda

Subphylum Crustacea

Number of species About 900 species representing 56 families in 6 orders

Size From a fraction of an inch to 10 in (25 cm) tall and 3 in (8 cm) in diameter

Key features Body form variable; sessile species protected by fortress of heavily calcified plates; curly thoracic feeding legs can be extended through "hatch doors"

Habits True barnacles are sessile as adults; smaller orders contain rock-boring and parasitic forms

Breeding Sessile barnacles are hermaphrodites and reproduce with close neighbors; larvae pass through 6 nauplius stages and 1 cyprid settlement stage before metamorphosing into adults; life span can be up to 10 years

Diet Sessile species are omnivorous suspension feeders, eating all manner of detritus; parasites feed on tissues and body fluids of host

Habitat Marine, from high tide mark on rocky shores to deepest ocean trenches

Distribution Found in all oceans and adjoining seas

Copepods

A female *Cyclops* with full egg sacs on either side of her abdomen. Although only tiny, *Cyclops* sp. copepods are predaceous and can capture relatively large prey, including the larvae of other crustaceans.
Length 0.04 inches (1 mm).

♀ *Cyclops* sp.

Common name
Copepods

Subclass Copepoda

Class Maxillopoda

Subphylum Crustacea

Number of species Up to 10,000 species representing 220 families in 10 orders

Size Mostly 0.04 in (1 mm) to 0.2 in (5 mm); some larger parasitic species occasionally up to 12 in (30 cm) long

Key features Small, triangular body with wide head and tapering tail; antennae long; compound eyes lacking, but light-sensitive "naupliar" eye present; thorax bears maxillipeds; 5 other pairs of thoracic limbs used for swimming; swimming legs covered in dense hairs; females often carry egg masses on each side

Habits Free-living species swim in plankton; many species are parasitic

Breeding Fertilized eggs shed into water or retained in brood chambers attached to female; eggs hatch and pass through 6 nauplius stages and 5 copepodid stages before final molt into adult form; life span usually 6–12 months

Diet Planktonic varieties feed on microscopic algae; some species are predaceous and feed on other crustacean larvae

Habitat Mostly fully aquatic; pelagic (living in open seas) and benthic (bottom dwelling); also in freshwater habitats; occasionally in soil and water films

Distribution Worldwide

Mussel Shrimps

Cypridina mussel shrimps spend most of their time swimming. Large swarms can generate bright luminous clouds when disturbed, due to a chemical reaction involving the enzyme luciferase.
Size 0.08 inches (2 mm).

Cypridina sp.

Common name
Mussel shrimps

Class Ostracoda

Subphylum Crustacea

Number of species Over 7,000

Size Less than 0.04 in (1 mm) to 1.2 in (3 cm)

Key features Body tiny; completely enclosed within bivalved carapace; head has well-developed first and second antennae and mouthparts; thorax and abdomen vestigial; maximum of 2 thoracic appendages

Habits Some species swim, burrow, or climb; live on or near the water bottom

Breeding Parthenogenesis is common; eggs either passed into the water, attached to plants, or retained within carapace

Diet Most are filter feeders; larger species are scavengers or carnivores

Habitat Mostly aquatic in marine and fresh water; a few species survive on land or in temporary water bodies such as puddles

Distribution Widespread in the world's oceans, rivers, and lakes; also on land

Mantis Shrimps

Mantis shrimps of the genus *Squilla* are tropical and often brightly colored. Their awesome weaponry means they have little to fear from any other animal and no need for camouflage. Length 12 inches (30 cm).

Squilla sp.

Common name Mantis shrimps

Order Stomatopoda

Class Malacostraca

Subphylum Crustacea

Number of species About 400 species representing 17 families

Size From 2 in (5 cm) to 16 in (40 cm)

Key features Robust, often slightly flattened body; carapace small, only covering front half of thorax; second pair of thoracic legs modified into huge barbed, powerful, clawlike subchelae used for hunting; last 3 pairs of thoracic legs slender and stiltlike, used along with tail to support body off the sea floor

Habits Aggressive and bold; adults bottom dwelling, may burrow in mud or other soft substrate, or occupy dens in rocks and coral; larvae swim freely in open water

Breeding Male and female pairs come together for courtship and mating; female tends eggs and young larvae alone in a den

Diet Exclusively carnivorous and predaceous; prey includes mollusks, fish, worms, and other crustaceans, such as small crabs and shrimps

Habitat Exclusively marine, in warm intertidal and subtidal waters surrounding most tropical coastlines; usually in less than 65 feet (20 m) of water

Distribution Mainly in tropical and warm temperate zones of Atlantic, Pacific, and Indian Oceans, and adjoining seas; a few species live in cool temperate zones

Opossum Shrimps

The opossum shrimp *Mysis relicta* lives in freshwater or brackish lakes and lagoons throughout northern Europe, from northern Italy to Finland.
Length 0.7 inches (20 mm).

Mysis relicta

Common name Opossum shrimps (fairy shrimps)

Order Mysidacea

Class Malacostraca

Subphylum Crustacea

Number of species About 800 species in 4 families

Size 0.1 in (3 mm) to 14 in (36 cm)

Key features Mostly small, shrimplike animals with a large carapace and a ventral brooding pouch

Habits Mostly pelagic (living in open seas); some benthic (bottom dwelling); some species form large swarms

Breeding Mating occurs at night; eggs and larvae develop in pouch on female's thorax and are released as small, fully formed juveniles

Diet Most species are omnivorous scavengers; some specialize in collecting tiny food particles that adhere to their body; others are predatory, feeding on freshly killed copepods and other tiny swimming, planktonic animals

Habitat Mostly marine, from intertidal zones to great depths; some species have adapted to brackish or fresh water

Distribution Worldwide

Sand Hoppers and Beach Fleas

Gammarus locusta is an amphipod from the lower shore. It is found under rocks among large seaweeds. Length 0.5 inches (13 mm).

Gammarus locusta

Common name Sand hoppers (beach fleas)

Order Amphipoda

Class Malacostraca

Subphylum Crustacea

Number of species Over 5,000 species representing over 100 families in 4 suborders

Size 0.04 in (1 mm) to 12 in (30 cm)

Key features Very variable in appearance; basic body plan for most is flattened from side to side and shrimplike, with no carapace; body may be protected instead by segmental armored plates; other forms are greatly elongated or spiderlike; 7 pairs of thoracic appendages, the front 2 used for feeding, the rest for walking; 6 pairs of abdominal appendages, the front 3 are pleopods, the rest stiff uropods; eyes small and unstalked

Habits Hugely variable; includes pelagic (living in open seas), burrowing, boring, tube-building, and commensal forms

Breeding Mating usually occurs in the water column with simultaneous release of male and female gametes and external fertilization of eggs; swimming larvae pass through several molts before taking on the adult form; development is rapid, and most adults only manage one attempt at breeding

Diet Most species are scavengers, grazers, feed on detritus, or are filter feeders; others are predatory or parasitic

Habitat Oceans, rock pools, beaches, estuaries, and fresh water and damp places on land; many live attached to another host organism

Distribution In all the world's seas, oceans, rivers, lakes, and streams, and on land close to water

Isopods

The sea slater *Ligia oceanica* is found in large numbers above the high-water mark on rocky coasts around Europe. It emerges at dusk and can often be seen scuttling over damp rock surfaces. This species is also known as the sea roach and occurs in North America from Maine to Cape Cod. Length up to 1.2 inches (3 cm).

Ligia oceanica

Common name Sea slaters
(sea roaches, gribbles), woodlice, and pill bugs
(sow bugs)

Order Isopoda

Class Malacostraca

Subphylum Crustacea

Number of species About 10,000 species representing 120 families and 9 suborders

Size Most 0.2 in (5 mm) to 0.6 in (15 mm), but can reach up to 16.5 in (42 cm)

Key features Segmented body with dorsal plates capable of overlapping to some extent; 7 pairs of walking legs; delicate abdominal appendages, used for swimming and respiration, are enclosed in land-dwelling species

Habits Bottom-dwelling crawlers; most can also swim; many burrow; some bore into wood

Breeding Mate after partial molt; females brood eggs and larvae in special chamber; young released at late manca stage or as miniature adults

Diet Mostly omnivorous scavengers and deposit feeders; some species specialize in grazing algae; woodlice eat rotting wood; a few large marine species are active predators of small invertebrates, and some families have blood-sucking parasitic representatives

Habitat Mostly marine, from tidal and estuarine zones to deep sea; also in fresh water and on land (pill bugs and woodlice)

Distribution Worldwide

Krill

Euphausia superba, found in the polar waters of the Antarctic, form vast swarms that can color the water red. Length up to 0.6 inches (1.6 cm).

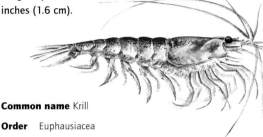

Antarctic krill
(*Euphausia superba*)

Common name Krill

Order Euphausiacea

Class Malacostraca

Subphylum Crustacea

Number of species About 90 species in 2 families

Size From about 1 in (2.5 cm) to 2 in (5 cm)

Key features Small, elongate, shrimplike animals; eyes dark and prominent; carapace covers entire thorax; first antennae each bear 2 long flagellae; second antennae have just 1; 6–8 pairs of thoracic appendages, each have 2 branches, with a long, bristly leg and a short flap with gills growing from the base of each; 5 pairs of abdominal swimming legs; tail segment long

Habits Adults form swarms up to several acres across and many feet deep; bioluminescence used to coordinate mass movement

Breeding Adults mate in midwater; fertilized eggs hatch into nonfeeding nauplii; many larval stages, each separated by a full molt

Diet Marine detritus, algae, and small planktonic animals, including other crustaceans

Habitat Mostly open seas, with a few species living on or close to the seabed

Distribution Global, in all major oceans and adjoining seas

Shrimps and Prawns

The common or brown shrimp, *Crangon crangon*, is an important commercial species found in the northeastern Atlantic and the Mediterranean. Length up to 4 inches (10 cm). The northern shrimp, *Pandalus borealis*, occurs in the North Atlantic, the North Pacific, and the Arctic oceans. It is a long-lived species, with a life span of up to 8 years. Length up to 6.5 inches (16.5 cm).

Common shrimp
(*Crangon crangon*)

Northern shrimp
(*Pandalus borealis*)

Common name Shrimps, prawns

Infraorders Penaeidea, Caridea, and Stenopodidea (Natantia)

Order Decapoda

Class/Subphylum Malacostraca/Crustacea

Number of species About 3,000 species, representing 3 infraorders and 2 suborders

Size Most less than 2 in (5 cm), but up to 14 in (36 cm) long

Key features Head and thorax protected by cylindrical carapace; head bears long first antennae, second antennae also have leaf-shaped scale; thorax bears 5 pairs of walking legs, abdomen has segmental swimming legs and tail fan

Habits Live in the open sea or near, or on the bottom of, the seabed; may form large swarms; many species migrate vertically each day to feed near surface at night

Breeding Males and females exist in most species, with female carrying eggs until hatching; some species are hermaphroditic; planktonic zoea larvae develop into postlarvae with full set of appendages, which in turn molt to become adults

Diet Scavenging omnivores

Habitat Aquatic, in marine, brackish, as well as freshwater environments

Distribution Worldwide

Lobsters and Crayfish

The European or common lobster, *Homarus gammarus*, is highly valued as seafood and rarely achieves its potential life span of 15–20 years before being caught by fishermen. The lobsters live in holes in rocks or tunnels beneath the sand and are found from the lower shore to a depth of about 200 feet (60 m) Length 18 inches (46 cm).

European lobster
(*Homarus gammarus*)

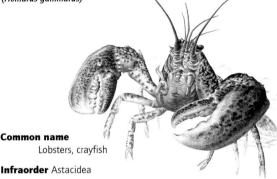

Common name
Lobsters, crayfish

Infraorder Astacidea

Order Decapoda

Class/Subphylum Malacostraca/Crustacea

Number of species Many hundreds in total, representing 7 living families

Size Usually up to 24 in (60 cm) long; occasionally 4.2 ft (1.3 m); the largest lobsters weigh over 44 lb (20 kg)

Key features Robust body with cylindrical carapace; abdomen long, slightly flattened, and segmented; first walking legs modified into large pincers (chelipeds); first antennae have two branches (biramous); second antennae shorter and lack antennal scales

Habits Nocturnal, solitary, and aggressive; several marine species migrate inshore to breed

Breeding Mating occurs after last molt; female broods eggs on abdominal pleopods; larvae are planktonic and settle as miniature adults

Diet Scavenging omnivores; nonpredaceous, but will grab anything that passes by; crayfish may also filter feed

Habitat Aquatic bottom dwellers; lobsters are marine, crayfish live in freshwater habitats

Distribution Worldwide

Mud and Ghost Shrimps

The flat-browed mud shrimp, *Upogebia affinis*, is a burrowing shrimp found in the Atlantic Ocean, Caribbean Sea, and the Gulf of Mexico. Length up to 2.5 inches (6 cm).

Flat-browed mud shrimp
(*Upogebia affinis*)

Common name Mud shrimps, ghost shrimps (glass shrimps)

Infraorder Thalassinidea

Order Decapoda

Class/Subphylum Malacostraca/Crustacea

Number of species Several dozen species representing 7 families

Size Can exceed 12 in (30 cm), but most species are much smaller

Key features Body long with compressed carapace; abdomen well developed; first walking legs modified into large, asymmetrical chelipeds

Habits Burrowing or commensal on other invertebrates, especially sponges

Breeding Females brood eggs and young larvae in burrows

Diet Marine detritus

Habitat Muddy and sandy seabeds; coral and rocky reefs from intertidal zones to deep ocean

Distribution Temperate and tropical oceans

Spiny and Slipper Lobsters

Panulirus argus, the Caribbean spiny lobster, is found—as its common name suggests—off the coasts of the Caribbean, the Bahamas, and Florida. Where the lobsters are not harvested, they can occur in very large numbers. Length 6-10 inches (15-25 cm).

Caribbean spiny lobster
(Panulirus argus)

Common name Spiny lobsters, slipper lobsters

Infraorder Palinura

Order Decapoda

Class/Subphylum Malacostraca/Crustacea

Number of species About 150 species representing 4 families

Size Up to 36 in (91 cm) long and 26 lb (12 kg), mostly much smaller

Key features Clawless lobsters with large antennae and spiny shells (spiny lobsters) or greatly flattened with reduced antennae (slipper lobsters)

Habits Nocturnal, timid, and generally solitary; occasionally undertake mass migrations

Breeding Female broods eggs on abdomen; dainty phyllosoma larvae are pelagic; postlarval stage is called a puerula; development is slow, but most species are potentially long-lived—up to 50 years

Diet Scavenging omnivores

Habitat Coral reefs and muddy areas of seabed, mostly in shallow water, but some down to 1,700 feet (500 m) or more

Distribution Tropical, subtropical, and warm temperate oceans

Squat Lobsters and Porcelain Crabs

The preferred habitat of the colorful spiny squat lobster, *Galathea strigosa*, is under mud, rocks, and large stones. It is found in the Mediterranean, the Atlantic, the English Channel, and the North Sea. Length up to 5 inches (13 cm).

Spiny squat lobster
(Galathea strigosa)

Common name Squat lobsters, porcelain crabs

Superfamily Galatheoidea

Infraorder Anomura

Order Decapoda

Class/Subphylum Malacostraca/Crustacea

Number of species Several dozen in 4 families

Size Carapace up to 5 in (13 cm); chelipeds up to 4 times as long

Key features Small lobster- or crablike decapods; 4 pairs of walking legs, first pair greatly enlarged; 1 pair of reduced legs at the back; abdomen tucked under body; porcelain crabs may have long, pointed rostrum

Habits Benthic (bottom dwelling) and pelagic (living in open seas); active mostly after dark

Breeding Mating occurs after a molt; eggs brooded on female abdomen; larvae pass through several zoeal instars before molting into postlarval form and settling as juveniles

Diet Omnivorous scavengers

Habitat Marine, from intertidal zones to deep water

Distribution Worldwide in temperate, subtropical, and tropical seas

Mole Crabs

The Pacific mole crab, *Emerita analoga*, lives on open beaches, where it buries itself in sand or mud. Dense populations of this mole crab species can be found in Peru and Chile. Length up to 2 inches (5 cm).

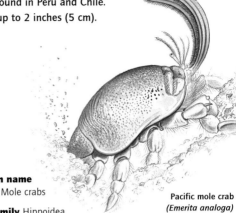

Pacific mole crab
(Emerita analoga)

Common name
Mole crabs

Superfamily Hippoidea

Infraorder Anomura

Order Decapoda

Class/Subphylum Malacostraca/Crustacea

Number of species Several dozen species in 2 families

Size Up to 2.5 in (6 cm) long

Key features Small, crablike body; fifth legs reduced; abdomen tucked under body; antennae long and feathery

Habits Adults burrow, remaining hidden between tides

Breeding Males often much smaller than females and may live attached to genital segment of female thorax; larvae are planktonic

Diet Filtered plankton and detritus, carrion, and soft tissues of stranded animals

Habitat Sandy beaches along surf line

Distribution Tropical and temperate oceans around the world; absent from polar regions

Hermit Crabs

Pagurus bernhardus occupies the disused shell of the gastropod *Buccinum undatum*. *Pagurus bernhardus* is the largest and most common of the northwestern European hermit crabs, occurring on all British coasts as well as south to the Atlantic coast of Portugal and north to Norway. Length 1.4 inches (3.5 cm).

Pagurus bernhardus

Common name Hermit crabs

Superfamily Paguroidea

Infraorder Anomura

Order Decapoda

Class/Subphylum Malacostraca/Crustacea

Number of species Several hundred species in 6 families

Size Most no longer than 6 in (15 cm); shell-less relatives may have carapace of up to 12 in (30 cm)

Key features Small, crablike animal; 4th and 5th pair of walking legs reduced; soft, twisted abdomen usually carried in gastropod shell; 1st legs modified into large chelipeds; 2nd and 3rd pairs used for walking; 4th pair used for grasping shell house from within

Habits Solitary and active; growing individuals upgrade to larger shells; fights over shells are common

Breeding Mating occurs out of shells immediately following female molt; eggs carried on abdomen inside shell and released as planktonic zoea larvae; larvae molt through several stages; when adult form is reached, they seek a shell in which to live

Diet Omnivorous scavengers and filter feeders

Habitat Mostly marine, from deep oceans to intertidal zones; some spend long periods out of water

Distribution Found in all the world's oceans and on land close to the sea throughout tropical zones

True Crabs

The shore crab, *Carcinus maenas*, is common in shallow water. It is a native of Europe, but has now spread throughout the world. Length 1.6 inches (4 cm).

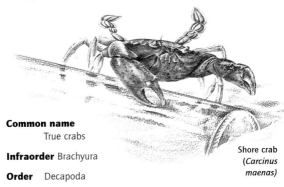

Shore crab
(*Carcinus maenas*)

Common name
True crabs

Infraorder Brachyura

Order Decapoda

Class/Subphylum Malacostraca/Crustacea

Number of species About 6,000 species representing 71 families

Size Carapace 0.1 in (2.5 mm) to 15 in (38 cm), leg span up to 13 ft (4 m)

Key features Short body with reduced abdomen tucked underneath flattened carapace; 4 pairs of walking legs, plus 1 pair of large claws

Habits Very varied; mostly nocturnal; may be solitary or gregarious; mostly aquatic and benthic (bottom dwelling); some swim well, others adapted to life on land

Breeding Mating occurs postmolt; females brood eggs under body attached to reduced abdomen; larvae pass through several zoeal stages and settle as postlarval megalops; a few land crabs skip the larval stage and develop directly into tiny adults

Diet Omnivorous scavengers of plant and animal material, filter feeders, and active predators of aquatic and terrestrial invertebrates, fish, and other animals

Habitat Marine, freshwater, and terrestrial habitats, including beaches, shallow and deep oceans, mangroves, coral reefs, rivers, lakes, estuaries, grassland, and forests

Distribution Worldwide

Sea Spiders

Pycnogonum littorale, the anemone sea spider, feeds by approaching the base of a sea anemone, inserting its proboscis into the anemone's soft tissue, and sucking.

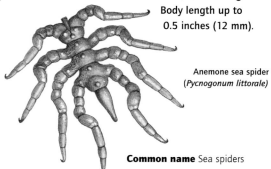

Body length up to 0.5 inches (12 mm).

Anemone sea spider
(*Pycnogonum littorale*)

Common name Sea spiders

Class Pantopoda

Subphylum Pycnogonida

Number of species About 1,000

Size From about 0.4 in (10 mm) to about 28 in (71 cm) across leg tips

Key features Color usually brownish, greenish, or yellowish, but sometimes brilliantly colored; body small and flat, divided into 3 recognizable regions: the head, the trunk, and the abdomen; the head is mainly distinctive for its unique tubular proboscis; 4 simple eyes; 8 long, spindly legs are attached to the trunk

Habits Most species live on the bottom of the oceans among hydroids and other marine creatures

Breeding The male clings beneath the female and fertilizes her eggs with sperm as they are released; he attaches the eggs to a special pair of appendages (ovigers) and carries them around until they hatch

Diet The main food apears to be hydroids, bryozoans, sea anemones, soft corals, and sponges; a few species feed on algae (seaweeds)

Habitat From the shallow waters of the lower shore to the deep oceans

Distribution In all oceans, including those in the polar regions

Horseshoe Crabs

The horseshoe crab *Limulus polyphemus* lives in water up to 75 feet (23 m) deep from the Gulf of Maine to the Gulf of Mexico. It spawns on shore in spring, and the eggs take a few weeks to hatch. The young are miniature replicas of the adults with a batonlike tail. Body length up to 24 inches (61 cm).

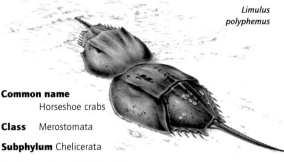

Limulus polyphemus

Common name
Horseshoe crabs

Class Merostomata

Subphylum Chelicerata

Number of species 4 (1 U.S.)

Size From about 2 in (5 cm) to about 24 in (60 cm)

Key features Body short and broad, tapering toward the rear, dull gray; divided into 2 parts: a forward part (prosoma or cephalothorax) and rear part (opisthosoma or abdomen); large shell-like shield covering the cephalothorax, which has a compound eye on either side, plus 2 pairs of smaller, simple eyes (median and lateral); 6 pairs of appendages; body terminated by long spine called a telson

Habits Sea living, foraging for food on the bottom mud and ooze

Breeding Millions of individuals migrate to the seashore in a mass orgy of egg laying

Diet Small invertebrates such as mollusks, crustaceans, and worms

Habitat Open sea, except when breeding

Distribution Seas around North America and Asia

Scorpions

One of the largest scorpions found in Africa, the African emperor scorpion, *Pandinus imperator*, does not use its stinger to kill prey, but as a last resort in defense. Body length up to 4 inches (10 cm).

African emperor scorpion
(*Pandinus imperator*)

Common name
Scorpions

Subclass Scorpiones

Class Arachnida

Subphylum Chelicerata

Number of species About 1,500 (about 75 U.S.)

Size From about 1.6 in (4 cm) to about 8 in (20 cm)

Key features Body flattened, mostly brown, black, or yellowish, sometimes deep green; body broad at the front, tapering backward to a long, upwardly curved flexible tail bearing a hinged stinger at its tip; pedipalps modified into 2 large pincerlike claws; a pair of comblike structures (pectines) trails down between the last pair of legs; eyes tiny, 2 in the center of the cephalothorax, 2–5 more on each side; breathing via book lungs

Habits Mostly nocturnal, spending the day hidden in crevices, under stones or bark, or in burrows up to about 39 in (100 cm) deep; all species hunt other small animals; some species wander in search of prey, others sit and wait in ambush

Breeding Courtship is complex and consists of a "dance" performed by male and female; females give birth to live young, which assemble on their mother's back and are carried around for some time; some species are parthenogenetic and produce young without first mating

Diet Insects, other arachnids (especially scorpions), centipedes, millipedes, snails, frogs, toads, lizards, small snakes, birds, and small rodents

Habitat Most common in deserts; also present in mountains, rain forests, gardens, in and around buildings, and on the seashore; a few blind species in caves

Distribution Worldwide, but mainly found in warmer tropical areas; only 1 species as far north as Alberta in North America; absent from northern Europe except as an accidental introduction in buildings

Pseudoscorpions

Neobisium muscorum from Europe is found in moss and behind bark on trees. It preys on small invertebrates. Body length up to 0.1 inches (2.5 mm).

Neobisium muscorum

Common name
   Pseudoscorpions

Subclass Pseudoscorpiones

Class Arachnida

Subphylum Chelicerata

Number of species About 2,500 (about 350 U.S.)

Size Body length from about 0.08 in (2 mm) to about 0.3 in (8 mm)

Key features Tiny black, brown, yellowish, or white creatures that resemble scorpions without a tail; rear of body rounded; pedipalps clawlike and furnished with poison glands, usually held out to the sides; silk glands present, opening onto jaws; 2–4 eyes, but more often eyes absent

Habits Secretive predators mainly found under stones; able to walk forward, backward, or sideways with equal ease; silk used for making overwintering and molting cocoons; many species ride on the bodies of insects

Breeding Male and female perform "dance" as in scorpions, and female picks up deposited spermatophore; babies feed on a milklike secretion from the female's ovaries; after emerging, they ride on her back for a while; most species take several years to become adult

Diet Insects and other small invertebrates

Habitat Several species common in houses; main habitat is among moss and leaf litter, under stones and bark, in the nests of birds, bees, ants, and termites, and in beetle larval burrows; present in forests, gardens, deserts, caves, and on the seashore

Distribution Worldwide except in polar regions, often occurring in houses

Tailless Whip Scorpions

Phyrinus is found under stones and bark in Florida and the Gulf states. It is most active at night, when it sometimes comes into houses. Body length up to 0.4 inches (10 mm).

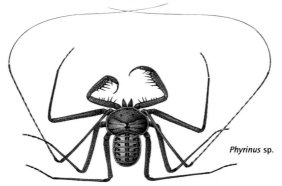

Phyrinus sp.

Common name Tailless whip scorpions (whip spiders)

Subclass Amblypygi

Class Arachnida

Subphylum Chelicerata

Number of species 80 (3 U.S.)

Size From about 0.2 in (5 mm) to about 1.7 in (4.3 cm)

Key features Flattened body, usually black, brown, or reddish-brown; often has paler spots or bands; abdomen joined to the unsegmented cephalothorax (which is wider than long) by a short stalk; usually 8 eyes in 3 groups, although sometimes 6, and in one case none; front legs very long and whiplike; pedipalps enlarged and spiny; no poison glands or tail

Habits Nocturnal predators that spend the day under bark or stones, scurrying off sideways when disturbed

Breeding As in true scorpions, the male guides the female over a spermatophore that he has deposited, and she takes it into her body; females lay 20–40 eggs in a lens-shaped sac attached to the abdomen; the babies assemble on their mother's back

Diet Insects and other arthropods

Habitat Mostly under bark or stones in humid places such as rain forests; sometimes in houses or caves

Distribution Only in the tropics and subtropics; in the U.S. restricted to the far south

Tailed Whip Scorpions

Mastigoproctus giganteus, the giant vinegaroon, is found in the southern and southwestern United States. It looks formidable, but it is nonstinging although it can spray formic acid in defense. This large whip scorpion is rarely seen since it only hunts in the dark. Body length up to 3 inches (8 cm).

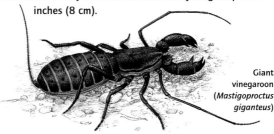

Giant vinegaroon (*Mastigoproctus giganteus*)

Common name Tailed whip scorpions (vinegaroons or vinegarones)

Subclass Uropygi

Class Arachnida

Subphylum Chelicerata

Number of species 85 (1 U.S.)

Size From about 0.6 in (15 mm) to about 3 in (8 cm)

Key features Body usually black, occasionally brown, fairly long and heavily built; carapace longer than broad; abdomen segmented, much longer than broad, ending in a long whiplike tail; pedipalps powerfully built and pincerlike; only 3 pairs of legs used for walking—the front pair twiglike and used as antennae; eyes very small

Habits Nocturnal predators that hide away during the day under logs, stones, or in burrows

Breeding Males generally bigger than females; the female is pulled across a spermatophore deposited by the male, who may then stuff the sperm packages firmly home with his pedipalps; female carries her eggs in a sac below the abdomen; hatchlings assemble on their mother's back

Diet Insects and other arthropods; frogs, small lizards, and snakes

Habitat Mainly under stones and logs in forests, also in deserts; some species come into houses

Distribution Mainly tropical, mostly occurring in Southeast Asia; 1 U.S. species in the far south

Mites and Ticks

As its common name suggests, the hedgehog tick, *Ixodes hexagonus* from Europe, is numerous on hedgehogs. A heavy infestation, particularly on young hedgehogs, can cause problems. Body length up to 0.3 inches (7 mm).

Hedgehog tick (*Ixodes hexagonus*)

Common name
Mites and ticks

Subclass Acari

Class Arachnida

Subphylum Chelicerata

Number of species About 45,000 (8,000+ U.S.)

Size Body length from about 0.003 in (0.08 mm) to about 0.6 in (15 mm)

Key features Body mainly black or brown, but many species red, green, or yellow; no division into cephalothorax and abdomen; pedipalps small, simple, and leglike; usually 4 pairs of walking legs; no tail or other appendages on abdomen; larvae have only 6 legs

Habits Many mites are free living in soil, on plants, or in both fresh and salt water; others develop within plants or on the bodies of animals; all ticks are parasitic on mammals, birds, and reptiles

Breeding Males may fight over access to females; sperm is transferred to the females by both direct and indirect methods; eggs hatch as 6-legged larvae, which molt to become 8-legged nymphs; females of many ticks lay several thousand eggs; ticks may need to use more than 1 kind of host in order to complete their life cycle

Diet Mites feed on all kinds of vegetable and animal materials; gall-forming mites are often restricted to a single genus or species of host plant; many mites take solid food; all ticks feed on blood

Habitat In soil, on plants, and on living animals in every conceivable type of habitat

Distribution Worldwide, including the deep seas and the polar regions; mites are probably the most ubiquitous of all animals

Sun Spiders

There are 25 different species of *Solpuga* in South Africa some of which are found in the Kruger National Park. The females dig burrows to lay their eggs. Body length up to 1.2 inches (3 cm).

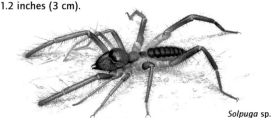

Solpuga sp.

Common name Sun spiders (wind spiders, wind scorpions)

Subclass Solifugae

Class Arachnida

Subphylum Chelicerata

Number of species About 1,000 (about 120 U.S.)

Size From about 0.3 in (8 mm) to about 2.5 in (6.4 cm)

Key features Body very hairy, usually reddish-brown or yellowish; abdomen long, soft, and elongate-oval, with 10 conspicuous segments connected to the cephalothorax via a waistlike constriction; chelicerae large and pincerlike; 2 small eyes on the front edge of the cephalothorax; pedipalps long, slender, and unmodified

Habits Mainly desert living, usually nocturnal predators with a good bit of speed on their long legs; they hide during the day under stones, bark, or in burrows

Breeding Male seizes female without courtship and transfers sperm manually; females lay about 50 eggs in burrows in the ground and guard the eggs and babies until their first molt

Diet Insects, other arachnids (including scorpions), centipedes, small snakes, lizards, birds, and rodents

Habitat Mainly deserts and dry savannas

Distribution Over most of the warmer parts of the world, including southern Europe but excluding Australia; in North America mainly in the Southwest, but found as far north as southwestern Canada; single species from Florida is only one from eastern U.S.

Tarantulas

The Mexican red knee tarantula, *Brachypelma smithi*, is found in the Pacific Coast regions of Mexico. Body length up to 2.4 inches (6 cm).

Mexican red-
knee tarantula
(*Brachypelma smithi*)

Common name Tarantulas
(bird-eating spiders, baboon spiders, whistling spiders)

Family Theraphosidae

Suborder Mygalomorphae

Order Araneae

Subclass Aranae

Class Arachnida

Subphylum Chelicerata

Number of species About 1,000 (about 30 U.S.)

Size Body length from about 1 in (2.5 cm) to 5 in (13 cm)

Key features Large, abundantly hairy body; usually blackish or brownish, but sometimes bluish or purplish or boldly marked with orange, yellow, or white; 8 very small eyes forming a close group; legs thick and hairy, each with 2 claws at the tip and a tuft of hair on the underside; males longer legged than females and sometimes with brighter colors

Habits Active at night, spending the day in burrows or in cavities in trees; hunting performed by touch and via sensory hairs; no web built; eyesight poor

Breeding Males wander at night in search of females in their burrows; mating is brief, lasting only a minute or so; females not usually aggressive toward males; eggs laid in burrow or other cavity, sometimes carried around by the female; females are long-lived (20 years or more) and produce many broods

Diet Mainly insects; also spiders, millipedes, sow bugs (woodlice), frogs, toads, lizards, small snakes (including rattlesnakes), and occasionally small birds or mice; long periods without food are not harmful

Habitat Deserts, savannas, and forests, mainly at low elevations; often in houses in the tropics

Distribution Mainly in warm areas; absent from Europe; U.S. species mostly in the southwestern deserts, absent from the southeastern U.S.

Funnel-Web Spiders

The Sydney funnel-web spider, *Atrax robustus*, the most deadly spider in the world, burrows beneath logs and stones in cool places in eastern Australia. Body length up to 1.5 inches (4 cm).

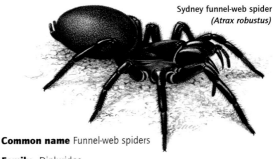

Sydney funnel-web spider
(Atrax robustus)

Common name Funnel-web spiders

Family Dipluridae

Suborder Mygalomorphae

Order Araneae

Subclass Aranae

Class Arachnida

Subphylum Chelicerata

Number of species About 250 (about 10 U.S.)

Size Body length from about 0.1 in (3 mm) to about 2 in (5 cm)

Key features Easily recognized by the long, widely separated spinnerets, which can be half the length of the abdomen or more; body mainly brown or black, rather long and flat; 8 small eyes grouped closely together on a slightly raised tubercle

Habits Web a broad, rather untidy sheet of dense, clothlike silk, often with a bluish tinge; usually placed among tree roots, in crevices in fallen trees, or among rocks; the spider waits in a tube set to one side of the web; some species can be aggressive and dangerous

Breeding Males (which are only slightly smaller than females) leave their webs and wander in search of females at night; female usually lays eggs within the web's retreat, but in some species she carries them around with her

Diet Insects, spiders, millipedes, worms, woodlice (sow bugs), and snails; larger funnel-web spiders can tackle frogs and lizards

Habitat Woodlands, mainly among the mossy base of trees, but also among rocks or on tree trunks; some species found in gardens; several eyeless species live in caves

Distribution Mainly tropical and subtropical, but a few species in southern Europe (Spain) and North America

Purse-Web Spiders

Atypus affinis builds its tubular web, the greater part of which is underground, in chalky or sandy soils that crumble easily. Body length up to 0.6 inches (15 mm).

Common name Purse-web spiders

Family Atypidae

Suborder Mygalomorphae

Order Araneae

Subclass Aranae

Class Arachnida

Subphylum Chelicerata

Atypus affinis

Number of species About 30 (8 U.S.)

Size From about 0.4 in (10 mm) to about 1.2 in (3 cm)

Key features Stoutly constructed, smooth, velvety, brown or black body; legs relatively short; chelicerae massively built, projecting well forward of the head; 8 tiny eyes grouped together; fangs large

Habits Females spend their entire lives inside a fingerlike tube or "purse web" that may be sealed at both ends; the tube can be hidden completely beneath a stone or project partly up into the open, often camouflaged with bits of leaf or twig

Breeding Males are about one-third shorter than females and more lightly built; they wander in search of female tubes and enter them for mating; females are extremely long-lived and lay many batches of eggs

Diet Mainly crawling insects; also sow bugs (woodlice)

Habitat Woodlands, swamps, and grassland

Distribution Locally distributed in Europe, Asia, Africa, and North America

Net-Casting Spiders

Deinopis guatemalensis, a tropical species, hangs above its insect prey, preparing to drop its net over an unsuspecting bug. Body length up to 0.8 inches (20 mm).

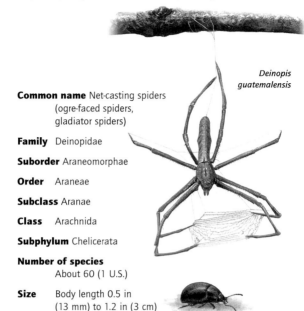

Deinopis guatemalensis

Common name Net-casting spiders (ogre-faced spiders, gladiator spiders)

Family Deinopidae

Suborder Araneomorphae

Order Araneae

Subclass Aranae

Class Arachnida

Subphylum Chelicerata

Number of species About 60 (1 U.S.)

Size Body length 0.5 in (13 mm) to 1.2 in (3 cm)

Key features Body long, slim, and twiglike, usually light brown; in *Deinopis* the small, flat face is almost entirely occupied by 2 huge staring eyes, below which are 2 tiny eyes (plus 4 more on top of the carapace, making 8 in all); in *Menneus* all the eyes are small

Habits Active at night, holding a tiny web in their front legs; the web is thrown over prey as it passes; during the day the spiders resemble twigs

Breeding Males are slightly smaller and more slender than females, with extremely long legs; female *Deinopis* constructs a globular egg sac suspended on a long silken line beneath a leaf; the finished sac is camouflaged with bits of leaf

Diet Various insects

Habitat On low trees and bushes in woods, rain forests, grasslands, and gardens; often common in built-up areas, sometimes on walls and fences

Distribution Mainly in warm areas, especially Australia; only a single species in North America (Florida); none in Europe

Spitting Spiders

Scytodes thoracica has a distinctive general appearance with a domed carapace. Now found all around the world, it traps its prey by spitting a stream of "glue" over it. Body length up to 0.24 inches (6 mm).

♀ *Scytodes thoracica*

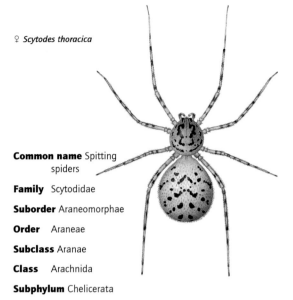

Common name Spitting spiders

Family Scytodidae

Suborder Araneomorphae

Order Araneae

Subclass Aranae

Class Arachnida

Subphylum Chelicerata

Number of species About 150 (about 8 U.S.)

Size From about 0.2 in (5 mm) to about 0.6 in (15 mm)

Key features Small, rather pale-whitish or brownish spiders, often covered in black spots; the shape of the carapace is unmistakable, being high-domed on top, sloping down more steeply toward the head; 6 eyes arranged in 3 well-separated pairs; legs long

Habits Wander in search of prey at night; immobilize victims by "spitting" a stream of adhesive liquid in a zigzag pattern across them; 1 species lives in large web complexes, but still spits when an insect arrives

Breeding Mating not preceded by any courtship; male simply walks onto the female's body and inserts his palps; the eggs are carried around by the female until they hatch

Diet Small insects

Habitat The commonest species is found worldwide in houses and backyards; other species live under bridges, beneath stones or rotting logs, among dead leaves, or on tree trunks

Distribution Worldwide for 1 species in houses; mostly tropical for species living in natural habitats

Daddy-Longlegs Spiders

The rafter or cellar spider, *Pholcus phalangioides*, is worldwide in distribution and can be found in cellars and caves. Body length up to 0.4 inches (10 mm).

♀ Rafter or cellar spider (*Pholcus phalangioides*)

Common name Daddy-longlegs spiders

Family Pholcidae

Suborder Araneomorphae

Order Araneae

Subclass Aranae

Class Arachnida

Subphylum Chelicerata

Number of species About 350 (40 U.S.)

Size Body length from about 0.08 in (2 mm) to about 0.6 in (15 mm)

Key features Legs long and slender, with flexible tips; body usually pale brown, yellowish, or gray; either 6 or 8 eyes, arrangement variable; male palp is large and simple in structure; epigyne (specialized reproductive opening) absent in females, replaced by a swollen zone

Habits Most species live in large, untidy webs slung in shady corners, on tree trunks, or under rock overhangs

Breeding Males and females often live together in the same web; males rather slimmer than females and with even longer legs; courtship virtually absent; female holds her eggs in her chelicerae; females and well-grown young often occupy the same web

Diet Insects and other spiders, including relatively large kinds

Habitat Some of the commonest species live in houses, cellars, and caves; many species live in the large crevices around the roots of trees in tropical rain forests, or under rock overhangs in deciduous forest; some prefer disused mammal burrows

Distribution Worldwide, inhabiting houses much farther north and south than the natural range

Crab Spiders

The common flower spider, *Misumena vatia*, awaits prey on a daisy. It is also found on goldenrod and other white or yellow flowers, giving it the alternative common name of goldenrod spider. Body length up to 0.4 inches (10 mm).

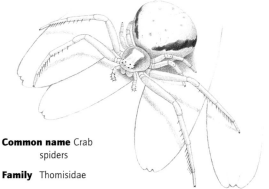

♀ Common flower spider or goldenrod spider (*Misumena vatia*)

Common name Crab spiders

Family Thomisidae

Suborder Araneomorphae

Order Araneae

Subclass Aranae

Class Arachnida

Subphylum Chelicerata

Number of species More than 2,000 (about 250 U.S.)

Size Body length from about 0.08 in (2 mm) to about 0.8 in (20 mm)

Key features Eight eyes, often on raised humps in 2 backwardly curving rows of 4 eyes each; body usually short and broad (but can be long and thin); back two pairs of legs often short and rather stumpy; front two pairs usually much longer and slimmer; each tarsus bears 2 claws; chelicerae lack teeth; venom usually very powerful

Habits Found on the ground, on leaves, or on flowers, usually remaining still for long periods in an ambush position; no silken webs built for catching prey; 1 species partially social

Breeding Males usually much smaller than females and normally a different color; mating generally takes place without any preceding courtship; during mating the male hangs upside down beneath the female, clinging to the underside of her abdomen; she may catch prey and feed while the male is thus occupied; females stand guard over their egg sacs, but often die before the babies hatch

Diet Most kinds of insects or other spiders

Habitat Almost anywhere: forests, grasslands, deserts, mountains, beaches, gardens, and houses

Distribution Worldwide, except the very driest and coldest areas

Jumping Spiders

Evarcha arcuata is widespread across northern Europe and can also be found in the southern parts of England. It prefers damp places and low vegetation, such as heather. Body length up to 0.3 inches (8 mm).

Evarcha arcuata

Common name
Jumping spiders

Family Salticidae

Suborder Araneomorphae

Order Araneae

Subclass Aranae

Class Arachnida

Subphylum Chelicerata

Number of species More than 5,000 (about 300 U.S.)

Size Body length from about 0.1 in (3 mm) to about 0.7 in (18 mm)

Key features Colors often very bright, especially in males; females normally drab and may even appear to belong to a different species; cephalothorax usually square-sided, often larger than abdomen; pattern of 8 eyes with distinctive large pair in center of "face"; other 6 eyes much smaller

Habits Active by day, usually seen wandering around on leaves, bark, stones, or soil in search of prey; a small number of species build prey-catching webs

Breeding Males often perform complicated courtship displays; eggs generally laid in a nest between leaves or under stones, guarded by the females

Diet Small insects and spiders

Habitat Everywhere from the seashore to the highest mountains and tropical rain forests to the walls and roofs of houses in New York or Los Angeles

Distribution Worldwide, but most common in the tropics

Lynx Spiders

Oxyopes heterophthalmus is found on low vegetation such as heather, where it lies in wait or chases prey. It is widespread in France, the Netherlands, and southern Europe. Body length up to 0.3 inches (8 mm).

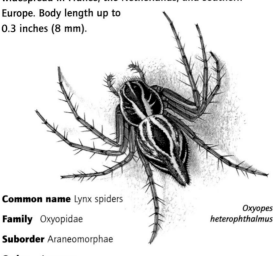

Oxyopes heterophthalmus

Common name Lynx spiders

Family Oxyopidae

Suborder Araneomorphae

Order Araneae

Subclass Aranae

Class Arachnida

Subphylum Chelicerata

Number of species About 500 (about 15 U.S.)

Size Body length from about 0.1 in (3 mm) to about 0.7 in (18 mm)

Key features Body mainly brown or green; cephalothorax high and oval; abdomen tapers off to a point; 8 eyes, of which 6 are arranged in hexagonal pattern with 2 smaller eyes below; legs distinctive, covered with numerous long spines that stand out at right angles

Habits Sit-and-wait or pursuit predators found mainly on vegetation; agile enough to leap up and catch insects in flight; use neither a web nor retreat except in *Tapinillus*

Breeding In most species mating is preceded by simple courtship; mating may take place suspended from a silken dragline; in 1 species male also wraps female in bridal veil; females sit and guard their egg sacs

Diet Insects; spiders, including members of own species

Habitat Mainly open places, meadows, savanna, desert, forest edges, a few species in forest

Distribution About 95% of species found in the tropics, but also U.S. and Europe

Wolf Spiders

In *Pardosa amentata* the males are similar in appearance to the female illustrated here, but generally darker with clearer markings. Body length up to 0.3 inches (8 mm).

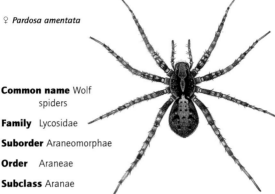

♀ *Pardosa amentata*

Common name Wolf spiders

Family Lycosidae

Suborder Araneomorphae

Order Araneae

Subclass Aranae

Class Arachnida

Subphylum Chelicerata

Number of species About 3,500 (over 200 U.S.)

Size From about 0.1 in (3 mm) to about 1.4 in (3.5 cm)

Key features Body mainly brown or gray, sometimes striped or spotted; cephalothorax and abdomen always longer than broad, often considerably so; eyes in 3 rows with 2 largest on top corners of "face"; long legs built for speed

Habits Many species run actively on the ground in daytime and have no retreat in which to hide, while a few live on vegetation; some construct burrows from which they emerge at night; only a few species use a web for capturing prey

Breeding Males generally use legs and palps to signal to female during courtship—some species generate sounds as well; females generally transport their egg sacs attached to their spinnerets; the spiderlings assemble on their mother's back and are carried around for a while

Diet Insects; other arachnids

Habitat From the seashore to high mountains; deserts, grasslands, forests, marshes, riversides, bogs, gardens, and roadsides; mainly on the ground

Distribution Worldwide, excluding the most hostile ultra-arid and permanently frozen zones

Wandering Spiders

A typical nocturnal wandering spider found in low vegetation and on the ground in the tropics and subtropics. *Ctenus* is found both in Africa and South America. This one from Uganda has a body length of 1.5 inches (4 cm).

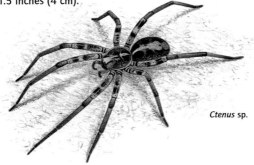

Ctenus sp.

Common name Wandering spiders

Family Ctenidae

Suborder Araneomorphae

Order Araneae

Subclass Aranae

Class Arachnida

Subphylum Chelicerata

Number of species About 600 (5 U.S.)

Size From about 0.2 in (5 mm) to about 1.4 in (3.5 cm)

Key features Small to large, mainly brownish nocturnal spiders with long legs; 6 eyes arranged in 3 rows, the 2 largest situated in the middle row and flanked on either side by 2 smaller ones

Habits Ctenids live on the ground or on vegetation, hiding away during the day and emerging at night to hunt; there is no web

Breeding Males may carry out vibratory courtship; the females of some species carry their egg sacs slung beneath the body, while in others the sac is attached to plants or hidden under stones

Diet Insects, frogs, lizards, and small snakes

Habitat Desert, meadowlands, scrub, forests, houses, and gardens

Distribution Mainly tropical; only 5 resident species in the U.S., mainly in the south; none in Europe

Nursery Web Spiders

In the wedding-present spider, *Pisaura mirabilis*, the color varies from gray to yellowish-orange to quite a dark brown. The abdominal markings may be striking or absent. This female is carrying a large egg sac under her body. Body length up to 0.6 inches (15 mm).

Common name Nursery web spiders

Family Pisauridae

Wedding-present spider
(Pisaura mirabilis)

Suborder Araneomorphae

Order Araneae

Subclass Aranae

Class Arachnida

Subphylum Chelicerata

Number of species About 600 (about 15 U.S.)

Size Body length from about 0.3 in (7 mm) to about 1 in (2.5 cm)

Key features Body large; mainly brown or gray, often spotted or striped with paler markings, resembling both wolf spiders and wandering spiders; 8 eyes of about equal size, arranged in just 2 rows and therefore quite unlike the pattern in other similar-looking spiders; legs long

Habits Day-active, mostly sit-and-wait hunters, with the exception of a few tropical species; often prominent on vegetation

Breeding In waterside species males court females by vibrating legs to produce ripples; in a single terrestrial European species the male presents the female with a fly; females carry around their egg sacs; most species make a nest for the hatchlings and then stand on guard

Diet Insects, spiders, tadpoles, and fish

Habitat Forests, meadows, grasslands, mountainsides, and gardens; rarely in deserts; many species on and near fresh water

Distribution Worldwide except in very harsh habitats

Sheet-Web Weavers

Agelena labyrinthica, the grass funnel weaver, can be found among low vegetation and makes a sheet web with a tubular retreat. Body length up to 0.6 inches (15 mm).

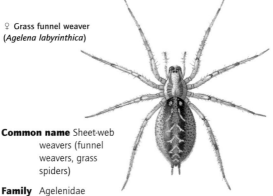

♀ Grass funnel weaver
(*Agelena labyrinthica*)

Common name Sheet-web weavers (funnel weavers, grass spiders)

Family Agelenidae

Suborder Araneomorphae

Order Araneae

Subclass Aranae

Class Arachnida

Subphylum Chelicerata

Number of species About 800 (over 300 U.S.)

Size From about 0.08 in (2 mm) to about 0.8 in (20 mm)

Key features Longish, densely hairy, brown or blackish-brown body carried on long legs that are abundantly spiny and hairy; usually 8 eyes in 2 horizontal rows; some cave species eyeless; a pair of peglike spinnerets protrudes from abdomen tip and so is visible from above

Habits All species build a broad sheet web with a funnel at one side; shady corners and hollows are often favored sites; prey will be attacked both by day and after dark; some of the larger species often wander around houses at night; 2 species are social

Breeding Males and females about equal in size; males enter females' webs and announce their presence by tapping on the silk; in some species males and females cohabit for long periods in the female's web; eggs are laid beneath bark or stones, or within an exposed silken nest

Diet Insects of all types

Habitat Houses, cellars, barns, outhouses, mountains, woods, meadows, marshes, and roadsides; in dark corners or on low bushes and among grass or rocks

Distribution Worldwide but usually avoiding very dry areas and absent from the coldest zones; more common in temperate regions than in the tropics

Comb-Footed Spiders

The mothercare spider, *Theridion sisyphium*, builds webs on bushes and other low vegetation with its retreat near the top of the web. Body length up to 0.15 inches (4 mm).

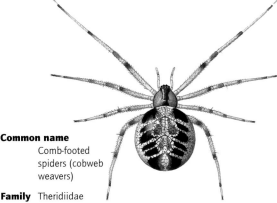

♀ Mothercare spider
(Theridion sisyphium)

Common name Comb-footed spiders (cobweb weavers)

Family Theridiidae

Suborder Araneomorphae

Order Araneae

Subclass Aranae

Class Arachnida

Subphylum Chelicerata

Number of species About 3,000 (about 250 U.S.)

Size Body length from about 0.08 in (2 mm) to about 0.5 in (12 mm)

Key features Abdomen mainly globular or flattened-oval, usually shiny and various colors; cephalothorax small; legs long and slender; 6–10 comblike bristles present on hind legs of most species; usually 8, but sometimes 6, tiny and inconspicuous eyes set close together in a group on the front of the head; cheliceral teeth absent

Habits Most species found hanging beneath untidy webs or suspended inside lair at top of web; a few species make single-line web or no web at all and hunt on foot; some species communal

Breeding Males often much smaller than females; courtship consists of tweaking of silken lines by male inside female's web, often accompanied by stridulation; females generally sit and guard egg sac until it hatches; may then look after the young, sometimes feeding them for some time

Diet Insects; other spiders

Habitat Every kind from forest and desert to houses and gardens; on or near the ground or in trees and bushes, under logs, in leaf litter, or in other spiders' webs

Distribution Worldwide except in driest and coldest regions

Large-Jawed Orb Weavers

Tetragnatha montana lives on low vegetation sometimes near water. It sits in the middle of its large orb web. Body length up to 0.4 inches (10 mm).

♀ *Tetragnatha montana*

Common name Large-jawed orb weavers

Family Tetragnathidae

Suborder Araneomorphae

Order Araneae

Subclass Aranae

Class Arachnida

Subphylum Chelicerata

Number of species About 600 (about 25 U.S.)

Size Body length from about 0.1 in (3 mm) to about 0.5 in (12 mm)

Key features Body long and narrow or relatively short and plump; brown, gray, yellowish, silvery, or green color, often (in *Leucauge*) with bright markings; chelicerae large, prominent, and projecting well ahead; male palps long and conspicuous; 8 eyes arranged in 2 equal rows; legs long and slender

Habits Most species build a horizontal or strongly slanted orb web, usually near the ground and often near water; a few species build no web and hunt among leaves or on the ground

Breeding Males and females are of similar size and look alike; mating habits vary; in some species males mate with newly molted virgin females; in others males enter adult females' webs and mate without prior courtship; females attach egg sacs to vegetation

Diet Insects of all kinds

Habitat Forests, meadows, marshes, roadsides, gardens, and sand dunes; often near water

Distribution Worldwide except in very dry or cold areas

Orb Weavers

Females of the wasp spider, *Argiope bruennichi*, have a quite unmistakable appearance, being large and strikingly colored. They build their extensive orb webs near ground level. Body length up to 0.9 inches (23 mm).

♀ Wasp spider
(*Argiope bruennichi*)

Common name
Orb weavers

Family Araneidae

Suborder Araneomorphae

Order Araneae

Subclass Aranae

Class Arachnida

Subphylum Chelicerata

Number of species About 5,000 (about 200 U.S.)

Size Body length from about 0.08 in (2 mm) to about 1.8 in (4.5 cm)

Key features Body shape and color incredibly varied; can be smooth or spiny, oval or elongate, flattened or spherical, brown or brightly colored; 8 small eyes arranged in 2 horizontal rows of 4; third pair of legs always the shortest

Habits Most species build an orb web and sit in the center or in a retreat to one side; webs usually sited in low vegetation, sometimes in trees; webs sometimes communal; some species build a reduced web, swing a prey-catching "bola" (a line weighted with a sticky blob of silk), or have no web at all and catch prey by sitting in wait like crab spiders

Breeding Males generally smaller than females, sometimes very much so; courtship usually consists of male vibrating threads of female's web; no courtship in some species with very small males; egg sacs usually placed among leaves or other vegetation, sometimes large and suspended like fruit

Diet Insects of all kinds

Habitat In every kind of terrestrial habitat; some species live in caves

Distribution Worldwide in habitable regions

Gossamer Spiders

Linyphia triangularis can be seen on any bush or plant with stiff foliage and on trees in woodland. It is sometimes found quite high up. Body length up to 0.3 inches (8 mm).

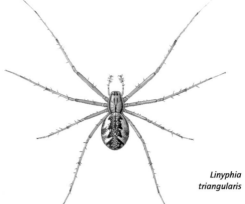

Linyphia triangularis

Common name
Gossamer spiders (hammock-web spiders, money spiders)

Family Linyphiidae

Suborder Araneomorphae

Order Araneae

Subclass Aranae

Class Arachnida

Subphylum Chelicerata

Number of species About 4,500 (950 U.S.), undoubtedly many more yet to be described

Size 0.02–0.03 in (0.6–0.9 mm)

Key features Body mostly black, sometimes with white markings, often dark brown or even red, shiny; more or less globular; legs relatively long and slender with long spines; 8 eyes in 2 rows; cave species often eyeless; stridulatory organs often present on the chelicerae

Habits Usually found hanging under a flat or dome-shaped web near the ground or in bushes; some species live on tree trunks, where they sit with their legs outstretched

Breeding Sexes often of same size; cephalothorax of male may be modified into strange shapes used during mating; male often cohabits with female in her web for long periods; male vibrates and plucks web during courtship; egg sacs placed in web or nearby

Diet Small insects

Habitat All terrestrial habitats from the seashore to the permanent snow line on mountains, in houses, caves, and the nests of mammals, birds, and ants; often abundant in woodland leaf litter

Distribution Mainly temperate zones, quite rare in the tropics

Neopilina

In 1952 the Danish research ship *Galathea* dredged up the first specimens of *Neopilina galatheae* from the Pacific Ocean. The species was thought to be restricted to the oceans around Central and South America, but in 1967 a specimen was caught in the Gulf of Aden in the Indian Ocean, revealing a much wider distribution. Size 0.04–1.2 inches (1 mm–3 cm).

Neopilina galatheae

Common name Monoplacophorans (*Neopilina*)

Class Monoplacophora

Phylum Mollusca

Number of species About 25

Size 0.04 in (1 mm) to about 1.2 in (3 cm)

Key features Limpetlike mollusks with a single, slightly cap-shaped unhinged shell; body flat and not spiral; creeping solelike foot; clear bilateral symmetry with some structures such as gills, retractor muscles, parts of the heart, reproductive, and excretory organs repeated one behind the other along the body; head reduced; few species alive today, many fossil examples

Habits Adults are marine bottom dwellers living in deep water

Breeding Little known; larval stage exists

Diet Unicellular organisms and organic detritus on the deep seabed

Habitat Limited distribution mainly in very deep marine habitats

Distribution Restricted, usually in the deep ocean

Chitons

Chitons tend to hide in crevices and underneath boulders, and are well camouflaged among the surrounding rocks. Their primitive "eyes" are embedded within their shell and are capable of detecting light and dark. Chitons will scurry away from the light when a boulder is overturned. Length 0.1 inches (3 mm) to 5 inches (13 cm).

Chiton

Common name Chitons
(coat-of-mail shells)

Class Polyplacophora

Phylum Mollusca

Number of species About 1,000

Size About 0.1 in (3 mm) to 5 in (13 cm)

Key features Adult body appears segmented with 8 overlapping shell plates; body not divided into segments underneath; head is simple and lacks eyes and tentacles; wide creeping foot on the underside; microscopic light receptors in the shell plates

Habits Marine, attached to and creeping on rocks and shells on the seashore and seabed

Breeding Sexes separate; sperm and eggs released into seawater, where fertilization occurs; forms a microscopic planktonic larva; larva matures and grows in the plankton, and at metamorphosis settles on suitable surfaces on the seabed

Diet Mainly herbivores, feeding on algae and tiny organisms; a few are carnivores; food scraped off rocks and hard surfaces using the radula

Habitat Seashore and bottom dwelling

Distribution All the world's seas, but better represented in tropical waters

Elephant's Tusk Shells

The elephant's tusk shell *Dentalium elephantinum* lies with its head buried in the sand. Its feeding tentacles are exposed. The animal's distribution ranges from Japan to the Philippines. Length up to 3 inches (8 cm).

Dentalium elephantinum

Common name Elephant's tusk shells

Class Scaphopoda

Phylum Mollusca

Number of species About 900

Size 0.2 in (5 mm) to about 6 in (15 cm)

Key features Tubular tusk-shaped shell open at both narrower (hind) and wider (head) ends; simple head with feeding tentacles; lacks gills; digging foot; mantle performs gas exchange

Habits Bottom-dwelling marine animals found at most depths; burrow in sediments

Breeding Sexes separate; microscopic planktonic larva forms after fertilization; settles on suitable sediments at metamorphosis

Diet Microscopic marine algae (diatoms) and larval and small juvenile invertebrates such as bivalves occurring in or on the sediment

Habitat Widely distributed marine sediments

Distribution All the world's seas and oceans

Limpets and Top Shells

Patella vulgata, the common limpet, is slow growing and can live for 15 years. It is found from northern Norway to the Mediterranean Sea. Length 2.4 inches (6 cm).

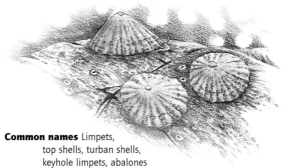

Common names Limpets, top shells, turban shells, keyhole limpets, abalones

Common limpet
(*Patella vulgata*)

Order Archaeogastropoda

Subclass Prosobranchia

Class Gastropoda

Phylum Mollusca

Number of species Unknown

Size 0.08 in (2 mm) to about 16 in (40 cm)

Key features Adult body usually asymmetrical and spiral (not obviously so in abalones and limpets); head normally with 1 or 2 pairs of sensory tentacles, usually with eyes, statocyst, mouth, and radula; well-developed creeping foot with sole; during development body organs and mantle may undergo torsion; bearing 1 flattened shell with apertures arranged in a row (abalones), a cone-shaped shell (limpets), or a spiral shell (top shells, etc.); shell usually lined with mother-of-pearl; head, body, and foot may be withdrawn into shell or covered by it; in top shells shell may be closed by an operculum; no operculum in abalones and limpets; 2 nephridia (excretory organs); well-developed mantle cavity housing ctenidia (gills) and osphradium (organ of scent detection) in some marine species

Habits Adults bottom-dwelling marine or freshwater animals; found in all depths in aquatic environments; foot used for creeping

Breeding Sexes separate; copulation may occur; fertilized egg develops into microscopic planktonic larva in marine forms

Diet Generally herbivores

Habitat Almost all marine, generally living on rocks, reefs, or other hard surfaces

Distribution All the world's seas and oceans; most common between the tidemarks and in shallow water

Winkles and Relatives

Littorina obtusata is known as the flat periwinkle. Its body shape is oval and flattened on top. It feeds on brown seaweed and is found across northwestern Europe from Norway to Spain. Diameter 0.4 inches (10 mm).

Flat periwinkle
(Littorina obtusata)

Common name Periwinkles, tower shells, conches, cowries, tuns, helmet shells, seasnails, slipper limpets

Order Mesogastropoda

Subclass Prosobranchia

Class Gastropoda

Phylum Mollusca

Number of species Unknown

Size 0.04 in (1 mm) to 18 in (45 cm)

Key features Adult body usually asymmetrical with spiral shell arranged in coils; head quite well developed, with 1 or 2 pairs of sensory tentacles, usually with eyes, statocyst, mouth, and radula; well-developed creeping foot with sole; during development body organs and mantle may rotate between 90 and 180 degrees in relation to the foot (known as torsion); shell may be closed by a horny stopper (the operculum) attached to tail of foot; body has 2 nephridia (excretory organs) and a well-developed mantle cavity housing ctenidia (gills) and an osphradium (organ of scent detection) in some marine species

Habits Adults mainly bottom-dwelling marine animals; some float on a raft of bubbles; locomotion is by creeping, using the foot

Breeding Sexes separate or hermaphrodites; mating may occur; fertilized egg develops into tiny planktonic larva in most marine forms

Diet Herbivorous and carnivorous

Habitat Almost all marine, generally living on rocks, reefs, or other hard surfaces

Distribution All the world's seas and oceans, most common in shallow water

Whelks and Cone Shells

Nucella lapillus, a dog whelk, is found on rocky shores in northwestern Europe. Height 1.2 inches (3 cm). The waved whelk, *Buccinum undatum*, is often found in waters of the eastern United States and Europe. Height 3 inches (8 cm).

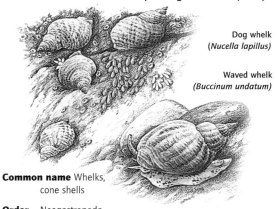

Dog whelk
(*Nucella lapillus*)

Waved whelk
(*Buccinum undatum*)

Common name Whelks, cone shells

Order Neogastropoda

Subclass Prosobranchia

Class Gastropoda

Phylum Mollusca

Number of species Unknown

Size 0.04 in (1 mm) to 18 in (45 cm)

Key features Adult body usually asymmetrical with a spiral, coiled shell; head quite well developed, with 1 or 2 pairs of sensory tentacles, usually with eyes, statocyst, mouth, and radula; well-developed creeping foot with sole; during development and growth the body organs and mantle covering them may rotate between 90 and 180 degrees in relation to the foot (known as torsion); head, body, and foot may be withdrawn into shell or at least covered by it; shell may be closed by a horny stopper (the operculum) attached to tail of foot; body has 2 nephridia (excretory organs), a well-developed mantle cavity housing ctenidia (gills), and an osphradium (organ of scent detection)

Habits Adults mainly bottom-dwelling marine animals; locomotion is by creeping foot

Breeding Sexes separate; mating may occur; fertilized egg develops into microscopic planktonic larva in most marine forms

Diet Generally carnivores, preying on various invertebrates; some cone shells can catch fish

Habitat Almost all marine, generally living on rocks, reefs, or other hard surfaces

Distribution All the world's seas and oceans

Bubble Shells and Allies

The attractive bubble shell *Acteon eloiseae*, Eloise's acteon, is found only in the Arabian Sea around the Sultanate of Oman. Length up to 1.5 inches (3.8 cm).

Eloise's acteon
(Acteon eloiseae)

Common name
Bubble shells, sea hares, sea butterflies

Orders Bullomorpha, Gymnosomata, Thecosomata, Aplysiomorpha, and Pleurobranchomorpha

Subclass Opisthobranchia

Class Gastropoda

Phylum Mollusca

Number of species Unknown

Size From 0.04 in (1 mm) to 8 in (20 cm)

Key features A diverse group; adult body snail-like or sluglike, usually with some coiling; may have a delicate external shell, but shell is sometimes internal or absent; radula usually present; external gill sometimes present; body may be narrow or broad, often wedge shaped with a broad, solelike foot on the underside; edge of foot may be drawn out on either side to form a flap or winglike outgrowths known as parapodia; front of body usually bears 2 tentaclelike sensory structures, but head structures often appear reduced; some shelled forms have an operculum

Habits Marine, generally bottom dwellers; often live in shallow coastal waters and on shores, burrowing in or living on the surface of sediments

Breeding Hermaphrodites; sperm transferred from the male organs of one individual to the female organs of another by copulation; after fertilization larval animals emerge to develop in plankton before settling on appropriate substrate, e.g., alga, shell, or rock

Diet Generally carnivorous, feeding on a range of bottom-dwelling invertebrates

Habitat Widely distributed in most marine environments, especially coastal ones

Distribution Worldwide in seas and oceans

Sea Slugs

The sea lemon, *Archidoris pseudoargus*, is commonly found on northwestern European shores. It is a large, warty slug and feeds mainly on sponges. Size up to 5 inches (13 cm).

Sea lemon
(*Archidoris
pseudoargus*)

Common name Sea slugs

Order   Nudibranchia

Subclass Opisthobranchia

Class   Gastropoda

Phylum Mollusca

Number of species About 1,700

Size   0.04 in (1 mm) to 8 in (20 cm)

Key features Adult body sluglike; uncoiled and lacking a shell and operculum, although often bearing exposed tentaclelike structures; body may be narrow or broad, with well-developed, adhesive, solelike foot on the underside, often ornamented by gills and papillae; head bears 1 or 2 pairs of sensory tentacles arranged in various ways; no mantle cavity; there may be a ring of gills around the posterior anus or the upper body surface; sides may bear tentaclelike cerata; torsion reversed in adults

Habits   Marine, generally bottom dwellers; often in shallow coastal waters and on shores, especially among rocks and algae; sometimes in deeper water; a few are pelagic (live in open sea)

Breeding Hermaphrodites; mating occurs; eggs often laid in elaborate and conspicuous jellylike egg masses; larva emerges to develop in plankton before settling on appropriate substrate such as alga, shell, or rock

Diet   Generally carnivorous; often specialists consuming one particular prey type or species

Habitat Widely distributed in most marine environments, especially coastal ones; some occur in oceanic planktonic habitats

Distribution All the world's seas and oceans

Snails and Slugs

The great pond snail, *Lymnaea stagnalis*, is found in ponds and lakes throughout Europe and in the Baltic Sea. It is a scavenger and eats mostly plants, but also dead plant and animal matter.
Length about
2 inches (5 cm).

Common names Freshwater snails, terrestrial snails, terrestrial slugs

Great pond snail
(*Lymnaea stagnalis*)

Subclass Pulmonata

Class Gastropoda

Phylum Mollusca

Number of species About 17,000

Size 0.04 in (1 mm) to 7 in (17 cm)

Key features Lung formed from the mantle cavity; full torsion is usually reversed to some extent; shell present and body coiled, normally without operculum (freshwater and shore-dwelling snails); no shell and no obvious coiling (tropical slugs); shell present and body coiled (terrestrial snails) or reduced or absent, with body not obviously coiled (slugs); no operculum

Habits Aquatic (generally fresh water) and terrestrial; air breathing; terrestrial species found in damp or arid soils; often associated with vegetation and may hibernate in crevices in wood and stone; one group inhabits seashores and, like limpets, lives attached to rock surfaces

Breeding Hermaphrodites, but copulation, sometimes preceded by courtship, occurs; sperm transferred by special reproductive structures; eggs usually laid in egg masses on rocks, pond vegetation, or in soil; juveniles hatch from egg mass

Diet Herbivorous or carnivorous, using well-developed radula

Habitat Freshwater lakes, ponds, rivers, and associated vegetation; widely distributed in terrestrial environments; limited distribution in seashore environments

Distribution Subtropical and tropical seashores and on almost all landmasses worldwide

Mussels

The brown mussel, *Perna perna*, occurs naturally in tropical and subtropical regions, specifically on the Atlantic coasts of Africa and South America. On both continents it is cultivated for human consumption. Maximum length 4.8 inches (12 cm).

Brown mussel
(*Perna perna*)

Common names Marine mussels, edible mussels, fan mussels, date mussels

Family Mytilidae

Order Dysodonta

Class Bivalvia

Phylum Mollusca

Number of species About 250

Size Up to about 18 in (46 cm) (fan mussels), but many less than 4.5 in (12 cm)

Key features Adult body enclosed in 2 equal, almost triangular-shaped shells with hinge near the pointed end; shells sometimes ornamented with spines, scales, or hairs; hinge more or less without teeth; mantle opens on the underside, and its left and right edges are not fused together on the ventral side; inhalant and exhalant siphons not very well developed

Habits Generally live attached to hard surfaces using the byssus filaments spun from a special gland on the foot; some live in soft sediments with byssus attaching them to a buried stone or pebble (fan mussels); others bore into rocks (date mussels); some live in mud wrapped in byssus filaments (mangrove mussels)

Breeding Sexes separate or hermaphrodites; sperm and eggs released into the water via exhalant water current; external fertilizaton takes place in seawater, and a planktonic larva results

Diet Adults feed on suspended microorganisms and particles of detritus; free-swimming larvae feed on phytoplankton

Habitat Widely distributed in marine environments, mainly in shallow water

Distribution Most of the world's seas and oceans

Oysters

Crassostrea virginica, the eastern oyster, is roughly pear shaped, but members of the species vary in size and shape. The outside of the shell is dirty gray or brownish in color, and the inside is white except for the muscle scar, which is deep purple. It is found in the Atlantic Ocean from the Gulf of St. Lawrence to the Gulf of Mexico and the West Indies. Length up to 8 inches (20 cm).

Eastern oyster
(*Crassostrea*
virginica)

Common name
Oysters

Family Ostreidae

Order Ostreiformes

Class Bivalvia

Phylum Mollusca

Number of species About 40

Size Up to 8 in (20 cm), occasionally larger

Key features Adult body enclosed in 2 unequal shells, which move together by a hinge with reduced teeth; mantle opens all around the shell, and its left and right edges are not fused together; the inhalant and exhalant openings are weakly marked

Habits Nonburrowing marine bivalves generally living attached to hard surfaces such as other shells, rocks, and corals

Breeding Hermaphrodites—begin as male and change to female, then changing back to male again a number of times over seasons; sperm and eggs released into water via the exhalant water current, where external fertilization takes place; no courtship or mating behavior; planktonic larva results, which feeds in the plankton until settlement and metamorphosis; no maternal care

Diet Adults feed on suspended microorganisms and particles of detritus; free-swimming larvae feed on phytoplankton

Habitat Widely distributed in shallow marine environments, lagoons, estuaries, rocky shores, and reefs

Distribution Most of the world's seas and oceans except the polar regions

Scallops and Allies

The edible Atlantic Bay scallop, *Argopecten irradians*, is found in Atlantic waters in beds of eelgrass. Its ribbed shell is gray to reddish-brown in color. Length 1.5–4 inches (3.8–10 cm).

Atlantic Bay scallop (*Argopecten irradians*)

Common name Scallops, saddle oysters, wing oysters, file shells, fan mussels

Order Pseudolamellibranchiata

Class Bivalvia

Phylum Mollusca

Number of species About 60

Size Up to about 6 in (15 cm)

Key features Adult body enclosed in 2 unequal shells, which move together by a hinge with reduced teeth; mantle edges not fused together and open all around the margins of the shell; positions of the inhalant and exhalant apertures weakly marked; the foot may secrete byssus filaments; in some species the juveniles are attached to weeds and rocks but break free as they age

Habits Nonburrowing; usually living free as adults; juveniles may be attached to hard surfaces or weeds by byssus threads; some species can swim by flapping their shells

Breeding May be hermaphrodites, being male first, then female, but sexes separate at any one time; sperm and eggs released into water via exhalant water current, where external fertilization takes place; no courtship or mating behavior; larva lives among plankton until settlement and metamorphosis; no parental care

Diet Adults feed on suspended microorganisms and particles of detritus; free-swimming larvae feed on phytoplankton

Habitat Widely distributed in shallow marine environments

Distribution Most of the world's seas and oceans, usually in relatively shallow water

Freshwater Mussels

Anodonta cygnea, the swan mussel, is a common freshwater mussel. It originates in Europe, and its preferred habitat is the silty bottoms of rivers, where it lies half buried beneath the sediment. Length up to 9 inches (23 cm).

Swan mussel
(Anodonta cygnea)

Common name Freshwater mussels

Order Schizodonta

Class Bivalvia

Phylum Mollusca

Number of species About 1,000

Size Up to 10 in (25 cm)

Key features Adult body enclosed in 2 equal shells hinged together by a few teeth; the mantle opens on the underside, and its left and right edges are not fused together at the back; there are inhalant and exhalant openings; no well-developed siphons, except in *Dreisenia*

Habits Generally shallow burrowers

Breeding Sexes usually separate, but some hermaphrodites occur; sperm and eggs released into the water via exhalant water current; external fertilization takes place in the water, or eggs retained in the female's body and fertilized by sperm drawn in by her inhalant water stream; no courtship or mating behavior; in a few cases planktonic larvae may result; often developing embryos retained in female's body; sometimes developing embryos released when a suitable fish host passes so that the shelled larvae (glochidia) can become attached to its fins for distribution; otherwise no care of young

Diet Adults feed on suspended microorganisms and particles of detritus; free-swimming larvae (when they occur) feed on phytoplankton

Habitat Widely distributed in freshwater environments, rivers, canals, ponds, and lakes, sometimes among vegetation

Distribution Most of the world's continents

Cockles, Clams, and Razor Shells

The sand gaper, *Mya arenaria*, is found in European waters, the North Atlantic, and the eastern Pacific. It is harvested commercially in the United States for research and culinary use. Length about 6 inches (15 cm).

Sand gaper
(*Mya arenaria*)

Common name Lucines, astartes, hatchet shells, cockles, giant clams, venus shells, carpet shells, razor shells, soft-shelled clams, jewel box shells, wedge shells, piddocks

Order Eulamellibranchia

Class Bivalvia

Phylum Mollusca

Number of species About 4,000

Size 0.04 in (1 mm) to 4.3 ft (1.3 m)

Key features Adult body enclosed in 2 equal or nearly equal shells hinged together by a few large hinge teeth separated from distinct long side teeth by a clear space; head poorly developed; mantle edges fused together in the lower back, forming distinct inhalant and exhalant water openings, which are sometimes extended out as tubular siphons; many highly adapted to life burrowing in sediment; deep burrowers have long siphons

Habits Bottom-dwelling burrowing animals; almost all species are marine; found at all depths in seas and oceans

Breeding Hermaphrodites, with sexes changing from males to females with age and sometimes changing back to male again to repeat the cycle; sperm and eggs released into the seawater via the exhalant water current and siphon; fertilization occurs in seawater; no courtship or mating behavior; planktonic suspension-feeding larva; no care of young

Diet Adults feed on suspended or deposited microorganisms and particles of detritus; larvae feed on phytoplankton

Habitat Widely distributed on the seabed and between the tidemarks

Distribution All the world's seas and oceans at most depths

Nautiluses

The nautilus is the last of a vanishing line of cephalopods once abundant approximately 400 million years ago. *Nautilus pompilus* is known as the pearly nautilus. Shell diameter up to 10 inches (25 cm).

Pearly nautilus
(*Nautilus pompilus*)

Common name
Nautiluses

Order Tetrabranchia

Subclass Nautiloidea

Class Cephalopoda

Phylum Mollusca

Number of species About 6

Size Shell diameter up to about 10 in (25 cm)

Key features Conspicuous coiled, external shell divided into many chambers; outer surface of shell usually beautifully patterned, internal surface mother-of-pearl; adult body housed in the largest, newest chamber; older chambers help regulate buoyancy; head bears 80–90 suckerless tentacles protected by a hood; in males 4 tentacles are adapted to form the "mating arms" (the spadix); mantle cavity and siphon used in "jet propulsion"; mantle cavity contains 4 gills; eyes not as well developed as in squids and octopuses, and lack cornea and lens, functioning more like a pinhole camera; brain, statocyst, and nervous system also less well developed

Habits Adults are midwater predatory marine animals; found at various depths from shallow water down to 2,300 ft (700 m)

Breeding Sexes separate; mating achieved by the male transferring a packet of sperm into the female's mantle cavity using a group of modified arms; eggs laid on seabed; planktonic larval phase is present

Diet Carnivorous, relying on senses to detect mobile prey, which often includes crustaceans

Habitat Tropical seas from surface to midwater or near the bottom

Distribution Limited to certain parts of the southwestern Pacific Ocean

Cuttlefish and Squids

A *Loligo* species squid holds a captured fish in its jaw. *Loligo* paralyzes its prey with venom produced by its salivary glands. This squid is found in the warmer waters off the West Coast of North America. Length up to 8 inches (20 cm).

Loligo sp.

Common name Cuttlefish, squids

Order Decapoda

Subclass Coleoidea

Class Cephalopoda

Phylum Mollusca

Number of species About 400

Size Length (excluding tentacles) from about 1.2 inches (3 cm) to 65 ft (20 m)

Key features Adult body short and flattened (cuttlefish) or long and torpedo shaped (squids), both with side fins; external shell lacking, but represented internally by a thick calcareous "cuttlebone" (cuttlefish) or a thin membranous horny "pen" (squid); 10 arms, 8 are similar in form, suckered, and shorter (1 modified in males for mating), 2 are longer; mantle cavity and siphon used in "jet propulsion"; cavity contains 2 gills; well-developed eyes with cornea and lens; brain and nervous system present; well-developed statocyst for balance and chromatophores for color change and camouflage

Habits Many adults are midwater- or surface-swimming predatory marine animals; some squids live in very deep water

Breeding Sexes separate; courtship and mating occur; male transfers sperm into female's mantle cavity using arm with specially modified suckers; planktonic larval phase is present

Diet Carnivores; well-developed hunting behavior using camouflage; prey subdued by toxic saliva injected using beaklike jaws

Habitat Most marine environments; more common in shallow coastal and pelagic (open) oceanic habitats

Distribution All the world's seas and oceans at all depths

Octopuses

Hapalochlaena lunulata, one of several species called the blue-ringed octopus, is found in the Indo-west Pacific and Indian Oceans. It is extremely toxic and can inflict a fatal bite. Arm span up to 8 inches (20 cm).

Pacific blue-ringed octopus (*Hapalochlaena lunulata*)

Common name
Octopuses

Order Octopoda

Subclass Coleoidea

Class Cephalopoda

Phylum Mollusca

Number of species About 200

Size Arm span from less than 2 in (5 cm) to 33 ft (10 m)

Key features Adult body usually round and relatively short; shell usually lacking, but occasionally present or may exist as a reduced internal structure; no lateral fins; 8 arms, all similar in form and linked by a web of skin for part of their length; suckers arranged in 1 or 2 rows; mantle cavity and siphon used in "jet propulsion"; mantle cavity contains 2 gills; well-developed eyes; brain and nervous system present; well-developed statocyst for balance and chromatophores for color change and camouflage

Habits Almost all adults are bottom-dwelling, predatory marine animals; many are solitary; behaviors complex, including use of ink to distract predators

Breeding Sexes separate; male transfers sperm into female's mantle cavity using arm with specially modified suckers; female often guards her eggs; planktonic larval phase present in many species

Diet Powerful carnivores; prey includes crustaceans, fish, and sometimes other octopuses; toxic saliva injected by well-developed beaklike jaws to subdue prey

Habitat Widely distributed in most marine environments, more common in shallow coastal habitats

Distribution All the world's seas and oceans

Sea Lilies and Feather Stars

Feather stars prefer to live above the seabed, often congregating on vertical rock faces and sometimes perching on other animals. The rosy feather star, *Antedon bifida*, is found in northwestern Europe. Size about 6 inches (15 cm).

Rosy feather star
(Antedon bifida)

Common name
    Sea lilies, feather stars

Order   Articulata

Class   Crinoidea

Subphylum Crinozoa

Phylum Echinodermata

Number of species About 625

Size   From 0.1 in (3 mm) to 3 ft (1 m)

Key features Adult body cup shaped; upper side bears featherlike arms in multiples of 5; underside of cup attached to substratum by flexible jointed stalk (sea lilies) or has jointed, clawlike cirri in groups of 5 (feather stars); color varied, often black, brown, or red; featherlike arms have side branches (pinnules); tube feet in clusters of 3 on arms and pinnules and in rows on either side of a food groove; head and brain absent

Habits Adults bottom-dwelling marine animals; sea lilies attached to hard base by a flexible stalk; feather stars free living but grip rocks and stones with cirri; sea lilies can swim for short periods by coordinated arm bending

Breeding No mating; sperm and eggs released into seawater; fertilization occurs outside the body; eggs hatch into microscopic planktonic larvae that metamorphose and settle on the substratum attached by a stalk; sea lilies retain stalk into adult life, feather stars break free from attachment as they develop

Diet Filter feeders, feeding on plankton and suspended organic particles

Habitat Exclusively marine, living on rocks, reefs, or deep-sea substratum

Distribution All the world's seas and oceans at all depths

Starfish, Brittle Stars, and Basket Stars

Ophiarachnella incrassata is a brittle star found on the Great Barrier Reef of Australia. Diameter 12 inches (30 cm). *Pisaster ochraceus* is found on rocky shores from Alaska to Baja California. Diameter 10 inches (25 cm).

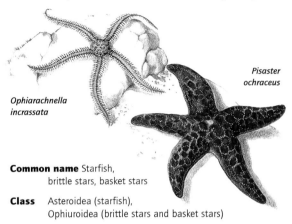

Pisaster ochraceus

Ophiarachnella incrassata

Common name Starfish, brittle stars, basket stars

Class Asteroidea (starfish), Ophiuroidea (brittle stars and basket stars)

Subphylum Asterozoa

Phylum Echinodermata

Number of species About 1,500 (Asteroidea); 2,000 (Ophiuroidea)

Size From 0.2 inches (4 mm) to 5 ft (1.5 m)

Key features Adult body star shaped; central body has 5 (occasionally more) arms; color varied, sometimes patterned; head and brain absent; no conspicuous sensory organs; flexible calcareous skeleton set in body wall; body surface covered in skin, sometimes decorated with spines; tube feet on underside of each arm, locomotion by tube feet (starfish) or arm movements (brittle stars and basket stars)

Habits Marine; adults live on seabed on rocks, reefs, and sand; normally lie with mouth against substratum; some burrow in sediments; movement in starfish generally by slow crawling using tube feet; brittle stars and basket stars move by flexing their arms

Breeding Courtship and mating absent; sexes usually separate; adults release sperm and eggs into seawater, where fertilization occurs; fertilized egg develops into microscopic larva that drifts in plankton; juveniles settle on seabed following metamorphosis

Diet Starfish are carnivores or detritus feeders; brittle stars feed on carrion, minute animals, detritus, or suspended food; basket stars are plankton and detritus feeders

Habitat Exclusively marine bottom dwellers

Distribution All the world's seas and oceans

Sea Urchins

Evechinus chloroticus is a regular (rounded) sea urchin with a mass of bristling spines and is found in rocky pools in New Zealand. Diameter 4 inches (10 cm). *Clypeaster rosaceus*, the brown sea biscuit, is very common around reefs in southern Florida, where it burrows just underneath the sand. Diameter 4.5 inches (11 cm).

Brown sea biscuit
(*Clypeaster rosaceus*)

Evechinus chloroticus

Common name Sea urchins, sand dollars, heart urchins

Class   Echinoidea

Subphylum Echinozoa

Phylum Echinodermata

Number of species About 950

Size   0.1 in (3 mm) to 7 in (17 cm)

Key features Adult body round, disklike, or heart shaped, showing 5-sided symmetry; colors varied, often black, green, gray, or brown; head and brain lacking; 5 paired rows of tube feet bearing suckers at tips; calcareous skeleton set in body wall (the test); test is usually rigid and bears mobile spines and minute grooming organs (pedicellariae) that may be venomous; many species have chewing organ (Aristotle's lantern) and teeth; long gut opens via mouth on underside and via anus on upper side of body

Habits Adults bottom-dwelling marine animals; usually lie with mouth downward; move using tube feet; spines used for defense and for burrowing in some forms

Breeding No mating behavior; sperm and eggs released into seawater; fertilization occurs outside the body; microscopic larvae generally planktonic; a few species brood their embryos

Diet   Algae, sea grasses, encrusting invertebrate animals, and organic detritus

Habitat Exclusively marine, living on rocks and reefs or burrowing in sediment

Distribution All the world's seas and oceans at all depth

Sea Cucumbers

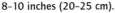

The sea cucumber *Pseudocolochirus axiologus* comes from the warm waters of the Pacific Ocean. Length 8–10 inches (20–25 cm).

Common name Sea cucumbers

Class Holothuroidea

Subphylum Echinozoa

Phylum Echinodermata

Number of species About 1,150

Size 0.1 in (3 mm) to 5 ft (1.5 m)

Pseudocolochirus axiologus

Key features Adult body cylindrical or cucumber or sausage shaped, occasionally very elongated or slightly flattened; colors varied, often black or brown, sometimes patterned; 5-sided symmetry evident in the number of rows of tube feet on the body; no distinct head; anterior mouth surrounded by a ring of specialized, retractable, branched feeding tube feet (oral tentacles); no brain; tube feet used for moving usually bear suckers at tips; calcareous skeleton weakly developed, set in body wall, which is usually soft and flexible and lacks ornaments apart from warts; no jaws; long gut opens via anterior mouth and posterior anus

Habits Adults bottom-dwelling marine animals; animal lies on its side; locomotion by tube feet or wavelike contractions; some forms live in crevices or burrows

Breeding No mating; sperm and eggs released into seawater; fertilization occurs outside the body; eggs develop into microscopic planktonic larvae

Diet Detritus and plankton collected by deposit- or suspension-feeding oral tentacles

Habitat Exclusively marine, living on rocks and reefs or burrowing in sediment

Distribution All the world's seas and oceans at all depths

Glossary

Words in SMALL CAPITALS refer to other entries in the glossary.

Abdomen region of an ARTHROPOD's body behind the THORAX

Alga (pl. algae) simple, nonflowering plant; largest examples are seaweeds

Androconia detachable scent scales on adult butterflies

Arthropod (PHYLUM Arthropoda) jointed-limbed invertebrate with hard-ended exoskeleton; includes insects, spiders, and crustaceans

Benthic living on or in the seabed

Bilateral symmetry symmetry in one plane, in which one side of an animal is an approximate mirror image of the other

Bioluminescence emission of light from living organisms

Book lung in arachnids a paired chamber in the ventral wall in which the gaseous exchanges of respiration occur

Bryozoan colonial marine organisms belonging to the PHYLUM Bryozoa

Budding form of reproduction in which small identical individuals (clones) grow from the body of the parent animal

Byssus threadlike filaments that attach some bivalves to rocks or plants

Carapace shield- or shell-like part of the exoskeleton; usually grows from the head

Cephalothorax combined head and THORAX, making up the front half of a spider's body

Cerci paired, articulated appendages at the end of the ABDOMEN; probably sensory

Chafer scarab beetle that feeds on leaves or flowers

Chelicerae the pincerlike first appendages found in chelicerates

Cheliped THORACIC appendage with pincers, often very enlarged. See THORAX

Chemosynthesis process by which certain bacteria use energy produced by chemical reactions to manufacture sugars

Chitinous made of chitin, a protein that is an important component of many invertebrate bodies

Chloroplast small organelle found in cells and containing the green pigment chlorophyll; site of PHOTOSYNTHESIS

Chromatophore cells in the skin of animals that can change color by contracting or expanding pigment

Cilium (pl. cilia) tiny hairlike projections growing from individual cells

Cirrus a slender, usually flexible appendage, e.g., an arm of a barnacle or a fused group of CILIA on some protozoans that functions as a limb

Clitellum the saddlelike region of earthworms that is prominent in sexually mature individuals

Cnidocyte specialized cell in cnidarians (members of the PHYLUM Cnidaria), used for capturing prey and in defense

Cocoon silken case constructed by the LARVA in which the PUPA is formed

Coelom the body cavity of animals whose body is made up of three layers; contains most major organs and is situated in the middle layer of cells

Commensal living in close association with another animal, not necessarily to its detriment

Copepodid LARVAL stage of copepods (members of the ORDER Copepoda)

Cornicle small horn

Cremaster structure at the rearmost tip of a PUPA, usually with tiny hooks to latch onto a silken pad spun by the caterpillar

Cydippid larva early free-swimming stage of members of PHYLUM Ctenophora

Cyprid late LARVAL stage of barnacle

Cytostome cell mouth in HETEROTROPHIC single-celled animals

Diatom single-celled ALGA that lives in the surface waters of seas and lakes

Dufour's gland gland in abdomen of some members of the Hymenoptera; may be involved in producing pheromones

Elytron (pl. elytra) thickened leathery, often hard, front wing of most beetles

External fertilization fertilization in which egg and sperm are united outside the mother's body

Extrafloral nectary nectar-producing structure positioned on a leaf or stem

Femur (pl. femurs, femora) third SEGMENT of an insect's leg

Fission reproduction in which the parent animal divides to give rise to one or more new individuals

Flagellate single-celled animal that has one or more FLAGELLA

Flagellum (pl. flagella) whiplike structure growing from a single cell

Frenulum in some members of the Lepidoptera a row of bristles on the front edge of the hind wings that joins the two pairs of wings together

Gamete reproductive cell (egg or sperm)

Gonads gland that produces GAMETES

Hair pencil cluster of hairlike scent scales usually tucked away within the body and protruded during courtship

Hermaphrodite has both male and female reproductive capability either simultaneously or as the result of a sex change

Heterotroph organism that takes its nutrients from consuming organic material derived from other organisms

Holoptic where the two eyes meet along the top of the head and almost touch

Instar the stage between molts of an ARTHROPOD

Internal fertilization fertilization in which the union of egg and sperm takes place inside the mother's body

Larva (pl. larvae) juvenile stage between egg and adult

Lek a grouping of males trying to attract females for mating

Lophophore tentacle-bearing, filter-feeding structure of certain aquatic invertebrates (such as moss animals, lampshells, and horseshoe worms)

Manca LARVAL stage of malacostracans

Mandibles the first pair of mouthparts situated on the head

Mantle special region of the body wall, particularly of mollusks, that encloses the MANTLE CAVITY and may secrete the shell

Mantle cavity space enclosed by the MANTLE, through which water circulates, bringing oxygen and taking away waste products. Contains the gills and the reproductive and excretory openings

Maxillae the mouthparts immediately behind the MANDIBLES

Maxilliped one of the first 3 pairs of THORACIC limbs of malacostracan crustaceans, adapted for feeding rather than locomotion

Medusa free-swimming form of animals in the PHYLUM Cnidaria

Megalops post-LARVAL stage of crustaceans in the ORDER Brachyura, in which the individual has full complement of appendages

Mesoglea middle layer of jellylike material between inner and outer layers of animals such as jellyfish and corals

Metamorphosis process of change by which one form develops into another, usually juvenile to adult

Mimicry ring group of SPECIES occurring in the same area and sharing a common warning pattern

Nauplius early LARVAL stage of some crustaceans, usually free-swimming

Nymph the LARVA of an insect whose wings develop externally

Ocellus (pl. ocelli) simple eye

Ommatidium single unit of a compound eye; acts as a light receptor

Operculum buttonlike plate on the foot of gastropod mollusks, used to close the shell after the body has been withdrawn

Osmeterium scent gland found in the caterpillars of swallowtail butterflies

Ovipositor egg-laying structure

Palp SEGMENTED, fingerlike structure forming part of the mouthparts in insects, usually used for touch or taste

Papilla small protuberance

Parapodia SEGMENTAL appendages of some worms, usually covered in bristles

Parasite organism living in or on the body of another (the host) and feeding on it for at least part of its life

Parthenogenesis production of young by a female without mating with a male

Pectinate shaped like a comb

Pedipalp appendage (usually sensory) on the anterior part of the body of horseshoe crabs, scorpions, and spiders

Pelagic living in open water

Pheromone a chemical scent that produces a behavioral result in another animal, usually to attract or repel members of the opposite sex

Photosynthesis the formation of sugars and oxygen by green plant tissues such as leaves when sunlight falls on them

Phylum a major group in the classification of animals, consisting of one or more CLASSES

Phytoplankton microscopic ALGAE suspended in surface water where there is sufficient light for PHOTOSYNTHESIS

Pilidium free-swimming LARVA of certain worms in the PHYLUM Nemertea

Plankton organisms, usually small to microscopic, that drift in the surface waters of rivers, lakes, and seas

Planula free-swimming early LARVAL stage of animals in the PHYLUM Cnidaria, including corals, anemones, and jellyfish

Pleopods paired abdominal appendages of certain aquatic crustaceans, usually adapted for swimming

Polyp SESSILE, tentacled form of animals in the PHYLUM Cnidaria

Predaceous describes an animal that preys on other animals for food

Proboscis tubelike feeding apparatus

Prolegs fleshy outgrowths in insect LARVAE that function as legs, but are not true articulated limbs

Pronotum protective shield covering the THORAX of an insect

Prothorax front SEGMENT of the THORAX

Protist animal of the kingdom Protista

Pseudopod flowing foot or needlelike cell extensions used by amebas and other members of the PHYLUM Sarcodina for locomotion and feeding

Pupa (pl. pupae) the stage (usually static) between LARVA and adult insect in those with complete METAMORPHOSIS

Radial symmetry many-fold symmetry around a single central axis

Radula small, horny, tonguelike strip bearing teeth, used by many mollusks for scraping food

Rostrum piercing mouthparts of a bug; it consists of an outer sheath with two pairs of sharp STYLETS inside

Schizogony asexual reproduction by multiple FISSION

Scutellum part of a bug's PRONOTUM that extends backward over the ABDOMEN; it is normally shield shaped

Scyphistoma larva POLYP-like asexual stage in the life cycle of jellyfish

Sedentary permanently attached, nonmigratory

Segment a section of a body part

Sessile unable to move around

Siliceous containing silicate

Siphon tube leading in or out of the bodies of invertebrates (especially mollusks), used to conduct water currents

Social living together in colonies

Spermatophore packet of sperm produced by male and delivered to female during courtship or mating

Spinneret silk-producing apparatus

Statocyst balance organ

Stridulate generate sound by rubbing one part of the body against another

Stylets sharp mouthparts modified for piercing skin or the surface of plants

Subchelae knifelike, recurved claws on the end of THORACIC appendages in members of the ORDER Amphipoda

Substratum(e) surface or sediment on or in which an organism lives

Symbiont organism living in mutually beneficial association with another

Tarsus (pl. tarsi) series of small SEGMENTS making up the last region of the leg of insects, the end bearing a pair of claws

Test external covering or "shell" of some invertebrates, especially sea urchins; lies just below the epidermis

Thorax (adj. thoracic) region of an insect's body behind the head; bears the legs and the wings (where present)

Tibia (pl. tibiae) fourth SEGMENT of an insect's leg, between the FEMUR and TARSUS

Torsion twisting of the body occurring in development of some gastropod LARVAE

Trochophore free-swimming LARVAL form of worms in the PHYLUM Annelida

Uropod flattened extension of the 6th abdominal appendage of malacostracans

Vacuole a fluid-filled space within the cytoplasm (living matter) of a cell, bounded by a membrane

Zoea larva early LARVAL stage of crabs

Zooid member of a colony of animals that are joined together; may be specialized for certain functions

Zooplankton small or minute animals that live freely in the water column

IUCN CATEGORIES

EX Extinct, when there is no reasonable doubt that the last individual of the species has died.

EW Extinct in the Wild, when a species is known only to survive in captivity or as a naturalized population well outside the past range.

CR Critically Endangered, when a species is facing an extremely high risk of extinction in the wild in the immediate future.

EN Endangered, when a species is facing a very high risk of extinction in the wild in the near future.

VU Vulnerable, when a species is facing a high risk of extinction in the wild in the medium-term future.

LR Lower Risk, when a species has been evaluated and does not satisfy the criteria for CR, EN, or VU.

DD Data Deficient, when there is not enough information about a species to assess the risk of extinction.

NE Not Evaluated, species that have not been assessed by the IUCN criteria.

Index

224